The Princeton Review®

CRASH COURSE FOR THE SAT®

6th Edition

princetonreview.com

Penguin
Random
House

The Princeton Review
110 East 42nd Street, 7th Floor
New York, NY 10017
E-mail: editorialsupport@review.com

Published in the United States by Penguin
Random House LLC, New York, and in
Canada by Random House of Canada, a
division of Penguin Random House Ltd.,
Toronto.

ISBN: 978-0-525-56914-5
ebook ISBN: 978-0-525-56915-2
ISSN: 1525-7177

SAT is a trademark registered and owned
by the College Board, which is not affiliated
with and does not endorse this product.

The Princeton Review is not affiliated
with Princeton University.

Editor: Orion McBean
Production Editors: Jim Mellon and
                    Emma Parker
Production Artists: Deborah Weber

Printed in the United States of America.

10 9 8 7 6 5 4 3 2 1

Sixth Edition

Editorial

Rob Franek, Editor-in-Chief
David Soto, Director of Content Development
Stephen Koch, Student Survey Manager
Deborah Weber, Director of Production
Gabriel Berlin, Production Design Manager
Selena Coppock, Managing Editor
Aaron Riccio, Senior Editor
Meave Shelton, Senior Editor
Christopher Chimera, Editor
Sarah Litt, Editor
Orion McBean, Editor
Brian Saladino, Editor
Eleanor Green, Editorial Assistant

Penguin Random House Publishing Team

Tom Russell, VP, Publisher
Alison Stoltzfus, Publishing Director
Amanda Yee, Associate Managing Editor
Ellen Reed, Production Manager
Suzanne Lee, Designer

The material in this book is up-to-date at the time
of publication. However, changes may have been
instituted by the testing body in the test after this
book was published.

If there are any important late-breaking develop-
ments, changes, or corrections to the materials in
this book, we will post that information online in
the Student Tools. Register your book and check
your Student Tools to see if there are any updates
posted there.

Acknowledgments

The Princeton Review would like to give a special thanks to Amy Minister for her extraordinary effort and expertise in revising this title.

Special thanks to Adam Robinson, who conceived of and perfected the Joe Bloggs approach to standardized tests and many of the other successful techniques used by the Princeton Review.

And last but certainly not least, the editorial team would like to extend a huge thank you to The Princeton Review's High School Content Director, Aaron Lindh.

Contents

Get More **(Free)** Content
at **PrincetonReview.com/cracking**

As easy as **1·2·3**

1 Go to PrincetonReview.com/cracking and enter the following ISBN for your book:
9780525569145

2 Answer a few simple questions to set up an exclusive Princeton Review account.
(If you already have one, you can just log in.)

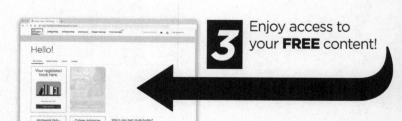

3 Enjoy access to your **FREE** content!

Once you've registered, you can...

- Access bonus math drills to practice the techniques that you will learn in this book.

- Download material for the optional Essay section, including style elements, a sample template, and practice prompts.

Need to report a potential **content** issue?

Contact **EditorialSupport@review.com** and include:

- full title of the book
- ISBN
- page number

Need to report a **technical** issue?

Contact **TPRStudentTech@review.com** and provide:

- your full name
- email address used to register the book
- full book title and ISBN
- Operating system (Mac/PC) and browser (Firefox, Safari, etc.)

Introduction

About this Book

If you're worried about the SAT, you're not alone. Your parents and teachers are probably driving you crazy with conflicting SAT information, so it's only normal to feel anxious. While the SAT is a very important test you should care about, The Princeton Review is here to assure you that reading this book is the first step to relaxing your nerves and feeling confident about the test!

This book will help you become acquainted with the SAT and improve your score on the test, all in nine simple steps that cover the Reading, Writing and Language, and Math sections of the test. We'll tell you everything you need to know about the content and format of the SAT and show you our proven strategies for increasing your score. After working through our nine-step crash course, you'll be a more confident and more prepared test taker.

What is the SAT?

The SAT is a three-hour-and-50-minute (with the optional Essay) standardized test used by many colleges as a factor in undergraduate admissions and placement decisions. The SAT consists of Evidence-Based Reading and Writing, Math, and an optional essay.

The test includes four sections in the following order: an Evidence-Based Reading section, an Evidence-Based Writing section, a no-calculator Math section, and a calculator-permitted Math section. Lastly, the optional essay section is at the end of the test.

The first section, Reading, takes 65 minutes and contains 52 multiple-choice questions based on 5 passages. There will be a short break before the Writing section, which takes 35 minutes and contains 44 multiple-choice questions based on 4 passages. Some of the passages in the Reading and Writing sections may contain graphs and figures. The Reading and Writing sections are used to calculate a single "Evidence-Based Reading and Writing" score on a 200–800 point scale.

The third section is a 25-minute no-calculator section with 15 multiple-choice questions and 5 grid-in questions. The final required scored section is a 55-minute calculator-permitted section with 30 multiple-choice questions and 8 grid-in questions. The two Math sections are used to calculate a Math score on a scale of 200–800.

As some colleges require that students submit essay scores, many students will stay for a 50-minute rhetorical analysis essay. The essay section will consist of a source text that you will be expected to read and analyze. You will need to write a response that explains how the author builds an argument based on evidence, reasoning, and stylistic elements. The essay is scored on a scale of 1–4 in three different categories (Reading, Analysis, Writing). Each essay is scored by two graders, and the scores are combined for a total score of 2–8 in each of these three categories. This essay score is a separate score and is not factored into your 200–800 Reading and Writing score. If you opt not to take the essay section, you may be given a short experimental section instead that will not count towards your score. Even if you take the essay, you may still have an extra section on your test. This means that some of the questions within the test, on that section or possibly elsewhere, are not counted toward your score. Just treat every question as if it is a scored question and do your best on it.

How Important Is the SAT?

Your SAT score is often one of many important pieces of your admissions portfolio. If your scores fall below a school's usual range, the admissions officers may look very critically at the other parts of your application; if your scores exceed the school's usual range, you will have a leg up on many others in the applicant pool. In general, smaller and more selective schools tend to place more weight on other factors, such as your interview, your essays, and your extra-curricular activities. On the other hand, larger schools (which have a very large applicant pool to choose from) tend to rely more heavily on SAT scores and high school grade point average. At these schools, admissions decisions may be based entirely (or almost entirely) on these two factors. This is not true, however, of every school; some schools have begun to de-emphasize the SAT, and a few have even made it optional. In addition, many schools no longer require the essay. Learn exactly what your preferred schools require by visiting the school's website or looking it up on our website, www.PrincetonReview.com.

What Is the PSAT?

The PSAT is very similar to the SAT. It is given by most high schools to students in their junior (and occasionally sophomore) year. The PSAT is used to help select National Merit Scholars, but unless you're one of the very few who are in contention for these scholarships, it's really only a practice test. Colleges will not see your PSAT scores; only your high school will. But if you're interested in doing well on the PSAT, all the techniques that you will learn in this book apply just as well to the PSAT as they do to the SAT.

What Will Each SAT Section Consist Of?

The Reading section of the SAT tests your ability to pick out facts from a reading passage. Two of the primary challenges in the Reading section are timing and endurance. Often SAT passages are quite dry, and 65-minutes of reading can seem tedious. In this book, we'll show you how to find facts in a passage efficiently with a technique that we've designed for the SAT.

The Writing and Language section of the SAT tests both grammar and style. You will not only need to spot errors in grammar, punctuation, and English usage, but also select answers that are precise, concise, and stylistically consistent with the overall flow and structure of the passage. This book will review the rules of grammar that you need to know and show you some helpful tips on how to identify the answers that express ideas most effectively. We'll also show you how to plan and write an effective essay.

The Math sections of the SAT put a heavy emphasis on algebra and algebraic manipulation. You will be expected to create, interpret, and manipulate equations in a variety of formats. You will also need to know how to identify the graphs of functions and find intercepts. A significant portion of questions will require you to interpret and analyze data from charts, graphs, and tables. Finally, concepts from geometry, trigonometry, and complex numbers will appear as well. This book will review the math that you need to know, show you easier ways to solve the problems, and help you avoid the College Board's trap answers.

What Is The Princeton Review?

The Princeton Review is a leader in test prep. Our goal is to help students everywhere crack the SAT. Starting from humble beginnings in 1981, The Princeton Review is one of the nation's largest SAT preparation companies. We offer in-person and online courses, as well as publish best-selling books in a variety of test subjects like the SAT, ACT, AP Exams, SAT Subject Tests, GRE, etc.

Our techniques work. We developed them after spending countless hours scrutinizing real SATs, analyzing them with computers, and proving our theories in the classroom.

How to Use This Book

This book covers the basic concepts and techniques you need to know to improve your score. Divided into nine steps, this book walks you through each of the three sections of the test, presenting important material and even drills to reinforce that material.

Read the technique chapters very carefully and do all of the drill exercises. Since the steps build upon each other, it's best to work through the steps in the order they are presented.

Because this book is a "crash course," it is intended to help you get the maximum improvement in a minimum amount of time. We won't waste your time going through every possible problem that might appear on the test. Rather, we'll teach you the essentials. If you have more time before the test, we highly recommend that you purchase our comprehensive titles *Cracking the SAT* or *10 Practice Tests for the SAT*.

Nine Steps

Why Nine Steps?

As mentioned before, we've divided this book into Nine Steps categorized by proven strategies used here at The Princeton Review. In the first two steps, we'll discuss some general strategies to help you get the best possible score on the SAT and introduce some techniques that you can use on every part of the test. Steps 3 and 4 will discuss the Reading, Writing and Language sections of the test, while Steps 5–9 will all discuss the Math section of the test. Some of our advice may be unfamiliar to you at first. You may even find yourself saying, "But my teacher would kill me if I did this on a test in school!" Just remember: This isn't school and if you picked up this book, you are trying to prepare for the SAT in a short amount of time. Trust us, our techniques are specifically designed to get you points on the SAT—and they work. Now let's begin!

Overall Test Strategies

Step 1: Pace Yourself

Most students think they need to do every problem on the SAT to get great scores, and they hurt their scores because they try to do too many problems.

It's very hard to finish every question while maintaining a high level of accuracy. During timed tests, people naturally rush—and they make careless errors and lose points. Almost everyone is better off slowing down, using the whole time allowed to work on fewer problems, and answering more of those problems correctly. You'll get a higher score if you do only 75 percent of the problems on this test and answer them correctly than if you do all the problems and answer about half correctly.

Here's how accuracy can help you: Let's say you attempted all 52 questions on the Reading test. If you answered 26 correctly and 26 incorrectly, you would earn 26 raw points for the correct answers. Let's say you slowed down and answered only 40 questions, getting 30 of them right. As you may know, the SAT does NOT deduct points for wrong answers, so you can simply guess on the remaining 12 questions (see Step 2). Odds are, you would gain some additional points for these random guesses—let's say 3 points. Overall, you'd earn 33 raw points. In this example, you did only 40 questions, but ended up with a higher raw score! Those 7 additional raw points could raise your scaled score by as many as 40 points.

For a better idea of exactly how many questions to do in each section to get the score you want, look at the following pacing charts. Notice that at all but the highest scoring levels, some room for error is built in, meaning you should try a few more questions than you need. For example, if you want to get a 600 in Math, you should try 45 questions, but you only need 39 raw points. Figure out how many more questions you need to get right in each section to improve your current score by 50 points. It's probably not as many as you think!

	Writing and Language Scale Score						
	10	**15**	**20**	**25**	**30**	**35**	**40**
10	200	250	300	350	400	450	500
15	250	300	350	400	450	500	550
20	30	350	400	450	500	550	600
25	350	400	450	500	550	600	650
30	400	450	500	550	600	650	700
35	450	500	550	600	650	700	750
40	500	550	600	650	700	750	800

Reading Scale Score (row labels at left)

Your verbal score is half Reading and half Writing and Language. As you can see in the chart above, for a 600 in verbal, you could have a perfect 40 on Reading and only a 20 on Writing and Language, or vice versa, or score a 30 on each, or any other combination that adds up to 60. Divide your target verbal score by 10, and your Reading and Writing and Language scores out of 40 need to add to that number. If one area is stronger for you, you can have a higher target for that section and not need to do as well on the other one.

For a Reading *Test Score* of:	You need about this many *Correct Answers:*	For a Writing and Language *Test Score* of:	You need about this many *Correct Answers:*
10	<3	10	3
12	5	12	5
14	7	14	8
16	10	16	10
18	14	18	13
20	18	20	16
22	21	22	19
24	26	24	22
26	29	26	25
28	33	28	28
30	37	30	31
32	41	32	34
34	44	34	37
36	47	36	40
38	50	38	42
40	52	40	44

To get: (scaled score)	You need to earn: (raw points)	Answer this many questions					
		Section 3: No Calculator		Section 4: Yes Calculator			
		15 questions MC	5 questions Grid-Ins	30 questions MC	8 questions Grid-Ins	Total # of questions to attempt	
350	12	5	1	9	1	16
400	16	7	2	11	2	22
450	20	9	2	13	3	27
500	26	10	2	18	3	33
550	32	11	2	21	5	39
600	39	12	3	24	6	45
650	44	13	4	26	7	50
700	50	14	5	29	8	56
750	54	15	5	30	8	58
800	58	15	5	30	8	58

Keep in mind that not every question is of the same level of difficulty. A hard question is worth no more than an easy question, so why waste time working on it?

Which Problems Should I Do?

You should do the problems that are easiest for you. In Reading and Writing, when you come to a difficult or time-consuming question, skip it for now. You can always come back to the question later if you have time.

Math questions follow a loose order of difficulty. The questions that come earlier in a section are generally easier than the questions that come later. However, this doesn't mean you won't ever find hard questions in the first half of a section, or any easier questions towards the end. If you come across a hard question early on, don't be afraid to skip it and move on! You may find some questions you like better even though they are later in the section. The order of difficulty resets with the grid-in questions; that is, even though the first grid-in question in section 3 is number 16, it is likely to be an easy question.

The most important question to ask yourself when you approach a problem on the SAT is this: How difficult is it? If it's an easy question, go ahead and answer it. If it's a medium or hard question, be careful! Try to avoid solving these problems in the usual way. Instead, use one of our techniques, or try to take a good guess using Process of Elimination (POE), which you'll learn about in Step 2.

Remember

Always ask yourself: Is this question easy, medium, or hard? Should I do this problem, and if so, how should I approach it?

Don't forget to guess on any questions that you don't get a chance to answer, though; you can pick up some extra points on these questions by guessing strategically.

Set Reasonable Goals

If you're currently scoring 500 in a particular section, trying to score a 650 right away will only hurt you. Instead, try to work your way up in easy stages. Pick a score range approximately 50 points higher than the range in which you're currently scoring. If you're currently scoring 500, aim for a 550; when you have reached 550, then you can aim for 600.

If you haven't ever taken a practice SAT, don't worry! The current SAT suite of assessments all use a common scale, so if you have your PSAT scores, you have a good idea of your SAT scores. The scale of the PSAT is from 320–1520, and the scale of the SAT is from 400–1600. The College Board says that this common scale means that a student who scored 500 in Math on the PSAT would also score 500 in Math on the SAT if they took both tests on the same day.

Slow Down

- Do fewer problems.
- Answer more problems correctly.
- Do the problems that are easiest for you.

Step 2: Learn to Use Process of Elimination (POE)

You don't have to know how to solve a problem in order to get the correct answer (or at least to be able to make a good guess). Aggressively using **Process of Elimination** (which we'll call **POE** from now on) will get you points on the SAT.

What is the capital of Malawi?

If you were to see this problem on the SAT (don't worry, you won't), you'd probably be stuck—not to mention a little upset. But the majority of the problems on the SAT don't look like the problem above. They look like the following:

What is the capital of Malawi?

A) Washington

B) Paris

C) Tokyo

D) Lilongwe

Not so bad anymore, is it? By knowing which choices must be wrong, you can often figure out what the answer is—even without knowing *why* it's the correct answer.

We'll discuss POE for each question type throughout the book, but the following are some key ways to use POE on the SAT.

POE on the Reading Test

There are two important rules of thumb to remember when answering Reading questions:

> - **Avoid extremes**
> - **Avoid offense**

The College Board does not pick extreme or offensive passages for its tests. If you see a choice that's very extreme (extreme choices sometimes use words such as *must*, *always*, *only*, *every*) or potentially offensive to a certain group of people, eliminate it.

Here are some examples of choices that you can eliminate, due to the words in bold:

- Disparage the **narrow-mindedness** of modern research.
- Judges **deliberately undermine** the Constitution.
- Doctors are the **only** people who can cure malaria.
- It was **entirely** misleading.
- **All** his beliefs about his parents were **wrong**.

Likewise, for questions that ask you about the author's attitude or tone, eliminate extremes, such as these:

- sarcasm
- ridicule
- repugnance
- condemnation

Authors are also unlikely to be confused about or uninterested in their own subject matter.

Which answers would you eliminate on the following questions?

43

Over the course of the passage, the focus shifts from

A) patterns in structural reef formations to similar patterns in oxygen levels.

B) wonder at an ancient marvel to a cynical analysis.

C) an illustration of a dramatic shift to relevant new research.

D) evidence gathered from examining trace metals to an exhaustive study of underwater fossils.

If you are looking to eliminate extreme answers, you are likely to get rid of (B), which contains the words "wonder" and "cynical." You might also eliminate (D), since it is unlikely that the passage can provide an "exhaustive study" (meaning a study covering everything) of any topic. Both (A) and (C) are reasonable answers, though, and there will be evidence in the text for one of them.

44

As used in line 57, the phrase "animals were indeed starting to fall prey to predators" implies that

A) most predators of the Cambrian were highly successful.

B) Ediacaran species were rapidly decimated.

C) *Cloudina* was an early species to evolve effective defenses.

D) researchers can infer whether predator-prey relationships existed millions of years ago.

Again, eliminating extremes can help here: the phrase "starting to fall prey" does not indicate that "most" predators were "highly successful" or a species was "rapidly decimated," which are more extreme than what the quote says. Cross out (A) and (B). While both (C) and (D) are possible answers, the "predator-prey relationships" in (D) more closely matches the idea quoted in the question.

We are not suggesting that you do questions without reading the text. We do, however, want you to keep an eye out for extreme, offensive, or unreasonable answers while you work through the Reading section.

POE on the Writing and Language Test

Getting rid of extreme answers and outliers can help on the Writing and Language test as well. Let's look at a few examples from a passage about Buffy Sainte-Marie, a Native Canadian singer-songwriter and activist. Which answers would you eliminate?

Sainte-Marie's music career **37**
has continued through today, with
her talents **37** featured on her
Oscar-winning Best Song "Up
Where We Belong."

A) NO CHANGE

B) shown up

C) zeroed in on

D) seen

Even without the full passage, you can probably tell that the tone in some of these answers is a bit off. Think of these passages as professional writing—the authors will not use slang to express their ideas if there is a more polished way to do so. For this reason, eliminate (B) and (C), then decide which of the remaining answers is best. (It's probably (A).)

Sainte-Marie's music career has continued through today, with her talents featured on her Oscar-winning Best Song "Up Where We Belong." 40

40

At this point, the writer is considering adding the following sentence.

> Many Canadian singer-songwriters, including Joni Mitchell and Gordon Lightfoot, also taught themselves to play guitar.

Should the writer make this addition here?

A) Yes, because it helps explain why Sainte-Marie taught herself to play guitar.

B) Yes, because it shows the link between Sainte-Marie's birthplace and her work as an activist.

C) No, because it provides background information that is irrelevant to the paragraph.

D) No, because it fails to indicate why Sainte-Marie chose to play guitar.

Again, the passage will provide more detail, but given the new sentence alone, ask yourself whether it seems like it would fit in an essay about Sainte-Marie. Does information about other artists add to an examination of her work? Probably not. Looking closer at the "Yes" answers also reveals some silly reasons for including the sentence. It does not explain anything about Sainte-Marie—it's not even about her! Eliminate (A) and (B), then use the passage to determine whether it's (C) or (D). Note that an answer like (C) is often right on these questions.

In short, Process of Elimination on Writing and Language questions can start with the following two ideas.

- Avoid casual language
- Avoid answers that aren't true

POE on the Math Test

There are two things to look out for in the Math section—trap answers and ways to estimate.

Avoiding Traps

Imagine that almost everyone who takes the SAT is *average*. Not stupid, but average. And when College Board test writers write the SAT, they write it in a very particular way. They write it so that the average person will get most of the easy problems correct, some of the medium problems correct, and none of the hard ones correct.

How do they do this? The test writers are very good at predicting what kinds of answer choices are attractive to the average person. They're good at it because they've been doing it for more than 40 years.

Average test takers always pick the answer that first attracts them. Attractive answers for math problems have nice round numbers that can be easily derived from other numbers in the problem.

Avoiding Trap Answers in Math

What does this mean for you? Before you choose an answer that just looks right, think about why it looks right, especially on questions later in the test that are generally harder. Do you know why it seems correct? If you don't know why it's right, but it looks correct, be careful! Often these are trap answers that repeat numbers from the problems, do simple addition or subtraction when more complicated math is needed, or are partial answers (answers that result from early steps in the problem solving before the final answer).

Take a look at this math problem.

20

Michelle rode her bicycle from her house to school at an average speed of 8 miles per hour. Later that day, she rode from school back home along the same route at an average speed of 12 miles per hour. What is Michelle's overall average speed for the entire trip?

A)   8

B) $9\dfrac{3}{5}$

C)   10

D) $11\dfrac{1}{5}$

Which choice do you think seems attractive at first? It might be tempting to see the numbers 8 and 12 and the word "average," and choose 10.

But this question is a question 20, so it's not likely to be quite that simple. The question didn't ask for the average of 8 and 12; it asked for an average speed of a trip, which is a more complicated concept. You may not know how to calculate it, but you should not choose 10 because that is the answer to a much simpler question than the one given.

Which other answer looks suspicious? Hopefully you said (A), 8. It doesn't make sense that her overall average speed could be one of the speeds she traveled. Also, the College Board will often try to trick you with familiar-looking numbers that come straight from the problem. The correct answer is much more likely to be one of the "weird" numbers we have left. (The answer is (B), but we're not going to spend time on why.) If you can quickly cross off a few choices on a hard problem and make a good guess, you'll be in great shape.

HINT

- Use POE and Avoid Traps.
- Guess aggressively.
- If you have no idea or have run out of time, just bubble in your favorite letter.

Estimation

On math problems, you may be able to use common sense and estimate an answer before trying to solve it. Often, several of the answers are unreasonable and can be eliminated right away. This will help you avoid careless mistakes and make good guesses, even if you can't solve the problems.

Read the following:

5

If 12 cans of food can feed 8 dogs for one
week, how many cans of food would be
needed to feed 6 dogs for two weeks?

A)   9

B)   12

C)   16

D)   18

Before you start to calculate, estimate. If 12 cans will feed 8 dogs
for one week, then 12 cans can feed 4 dogs for 2 weeks. Since you
need to feed 6 dogs for 2 weeks, the answer must be greater than 12.
Eliminate (A) and (B). The answer must be either (C) or (D). Now, if
you can calculate the answer, great. If not, you've got a 50 percent
chance of a correct guess.

You can estimate a lot more on the SAT than you might think, particularly on geometry. Estimate whenever you can!

We'll look at many more ways to use POE in the different parts of the
test in the following chapters.

Letter of the Day (LOTD)

Sometimes you won't be able to eliminate any answers, and other times there are questions that you won't have time to look at. For those, we have a simple solution.

Pick a "letter of the day," or LOTD (from A to D) and use that letter for all the questions from which you weren't able to eliminate any choices.

This is a quick and easy way to make sure that you've bubbled everything. It also has some potential statistical advantages. If all the answers show up about a fourth of the time and you guess the same answer every time you have to guess, you're likely to get a couple of freebies.

LOTD should absolutely be an afterthought; it's far more important and helpful to your score to eliminate answer choices. But for those questions you **don't know at all or intentionally skip,** LOTD is better than full-on random guessing or no strategy at all.

Verbal
Strategies

Step 3: Reading

Half of your Evidence-Based Reading and Writing score comes from the Reading Test, a 65-minute test that requires you to answer 52 questions spread out over five passages. The questions will ask you to do everything from determining the meaning of words in context to deciding an author's purpose for a detail to finding the main idea of a whole passage to pinpointing information on a graph. Each passage ranges from 500 to 750 words and has 10 or 11 questions. Time will be tight on this test. The purpose of this chapter is to introduce you to a basic approach that will streamline how you take the test and allow you to focus on only what you need to get your points.

Okay...so how do you get those points? Let's start with the College Board's instructions for the Reading Test.

DIRECTIONS

Each passage or pair of passages below is followed by a number of questions. After reading each passage or pair, choose the best answer to each question based on what is stated or implied in the passage or passages and in any accompanying graphics (such as a table or graph).

You might think that this means that you need to read the passage carefully, understand it thoroughly, or make complex inferences from the information contained in the passage. You don't.

Think of reading as a treasure hunt: All the answers to the questions are buried somewhere in the passage. All you've got to do is find them.

Approaching Reading

The problem with Reading questions is, of course, that these passages are boring, dense, brutish, and long. How can you get the most points in the least amount of time, and in the most reliable way? Well, not by reading the whole passage carefully. You can do it by knowing where to find the answer quickly within the passage, and then finding the choice that restates what is said in the passage.

An Encyclopedia

If someone were to give you a ten-volume encyclopedia and ask you the year of Pasteur's death, would you begin reading at the A's and work all the way through to the P's until you found Pasteur? Of course not. You'd go right to the entry on Pasteur and read only the five or six lines that you need. That's how you should approach Reading questions.

Your Treasure Hunt

So here are the steps to finding your answers in the most efficient way:

1. After reading the blurb, go straight to the questions. Do the line-specific questions first and the general questions later.

2. Make sure you understand exactly what the question is asking.

3. Predict the answer based on evidence from the passage. Underline that text.

4. Eliminate answer choices that don't match what you found in the passage.

Specific Questions

Many Reading questions will be line-specific questions. That is, they will ask you for facts from particular parts of the passage. Some of those ask you for the definition of words.

To answer any line-specific question, the method is the same. Hunt for the answer in the passage using the clues in the question, read that area of the passage to find the answer to the question, and then pick the answer choice that is the the the closest match to what the passage says.

The most common kinds of line-specific questions are line number and vocabulary in context questions:

- **Line number questions:** If the question gives you a line reference, go back to the passage and read that line in context (from about three to five lines before the line reference, to three to five lines following the line reference). Then, find the choice that restates what is said in these lines.

- **Vocabulary in context questions:** If the question asks you to define a word, go back to the sentence in which the word occurs and cross it out. Then, read the sentence and pick your own word to put in its place. This will give you an idea of what the word should mean. (Be careful, because the word in question may not have the meaning that's most familiar to you!) Then, look for the choice that best states what you think the word means in context.

POE on Specific Questions

When trying to find the answer that matches your prediction, don't forget about POE. On specific questions, it should be fairly straightforward to eliminate answers that don't match what you underlined in the text. If more than one answer remains, look for other reasons to eliminate one of them. As indicated in the last chapter, two things to avoid in Reading are answers that are too extreme and answers that are potentially offensive.

Your Turn—Exercise 3.1

Try answering the questions following the excerpt below.

Sleep deprivation experts have suggested a link between the amount of sleep a person gets and the likelihood of being overweight. A study conducted in Japan compared seven- and
Lines eight-year-olds who slept nine or more hours per night to those
5 who slept fewer hours than that. Those who slept eight hours were twice as likely to have weight problems as those who slept nine or more hours per night. The children who slept less than eight hours were four times as likely to be obese as those who slept nine or more hours per night. One theory suggested by dieticians to
10 explain this data is that sleep deprivation affects hormone levels. Another theory is that people who lack sleep eat high-sugar foods during the day for energy and may generally be lethargic due to a lack of energy.

The study cited in lines 3–5 ("A study . . . that") serves primarily to

A) explain how hormone levels affect weight gain.

B) indicate why some children lack energy.

C) support the theory discussed in the first sentence.

D) establish evidence to prove the theory in the last sentence.

2

It can be most strongly inferred from the passage that

A) increased sleep induces weight loss.

B) people should sleep ten hours per night.

C) dieticians have determined the causes of obesity.

D) not all Japanese children get the same amount of sleep.

Answers and Explanations to Exercise 3.1

1. **C** The study provides evidence that there might be a link, as stated in the first sentence. Because the passage does not explain the relationship between hormone levels and weight gain, (A) can be eliminated. Eliminate (B) because the study never addressed why some children lacked energy. While (D) is tempting, "prove" is extreme, and the theory is presented in the passage as a way to explain the study, not the other way around.

2. **D** Because the study was conducted in Japan, and there were two groups, each based on amount of sleep per night, it can be inferred that not all Japanese children sleep for the same amount of time. Eliminate (A) because while decreased sleep might be linked to weight gain, it doesn't follow that increased sleep induces weight loss. While (B) is tempting, be aware of the extreme word "should," as it is usually wrong unless the author specifically recommends a course of action. Choice (C) is incorrect because the dieticians present at least two theories to explain obesity but have not determined the causes.

General Questions

You may see one or two general questions that ask you for the main point or primary purpose of the passage. Save these for last; after answering the line-specific questions, you'll almost always have a good sense of the main idea. If you're stuck, try rereading the blurb, the first and last lines of every paragraph, and any line that contains a trigger word (*but, yet, although, nevertheless, however*). These are the most important lines in the passage, and you will most likely find the main idea in these lines.

POE on General Questions

We talked a little about POE on Specific Questions in the last chapter. The two biggest pitfalls to avoid on general questions are as follows:

- The choice is too specific.
- The choice describes something impossible to accomplish.

Choices that are discussed only in one part of the passage are too specific to be the main point. The main point of a passage is something that relates to the passage as a whole. Also, use common sense: any choice that is impossible to accomplish in a couple of paragraphs (such as "prove that comets killed the dinosaurs") can't be the answer to a general question.

Try these techniques on the following passage:

John Dewey was an American educator and thinker. In the following excerpt from *Democracy and Education,* he explains why education is necessary for human beings.

The most notable distinction between living and inanimate things is that the former maintain themselves by renewal. A stone when struck resists. If its resistance is greater than the force of the blow struck, it remains outwardly unchanged. Otherwise, it is shattered into smaller bits. Never does the stone attempt to react in such a way that it may maintain itself against the blow, much less so as to render the blow a contributing factor to its own continued action. While the living thing may easily be crushed by superior force, it nonetheless tries to turn the energies that act upon it into means of its own further existence. If it cannot do so, it does not just split into smaller pieces (at least in the higher forms of life), but loses its identity as a living thing. As long as it endures, the living thing struggles to use surrounding energies in its own behalf. It uses light, air, moisture, and the material of soil. Life is a self-renewing process through action upon the environment.

With the renewal of physical existence goes, in the case of human beings, the recreation of beliefs, ideals, hopes, happiness, misery, and practices. The continuity of any experience, through renewing of the social group, is a literal fact. Education, in its broadest sense, is the means of this social continuity of life. Every one of the constituent elements of a social group, in a modern city as in a savage tribe, is born immature, helpless, without language, beliefs, ideas, or social standards. Each individual, each unit who is the carrier of the life-experience of his group, in time passes away. Yet the life of the group goes on.

The primary ineluctable facts of the birth and death of each one of the constituent members in a social group determine the necessity of education. Even in a savage tribe, the achievements of adults are far beyond what the immature members would be capable of if left to themselves. With the growth of civilization, the gap between the original capacities of the immature and the

standards and customs of the elders increases. Mere physical growing up, mere mastery of the bare necessities of subsistence will not suffice to reproduce the life of the group. Deliberate effort
35 and the taking of thoughtful pains are required. Beings who are born not only unaware of, but quite indifferent to, the aims and habits of the social group have to be rendered cognizant of them and actively interested. Education, and education alone, spans the gap.
40   Society exists through a process of transmission quite similar to biological life. Without this communication of ideals, hopes, expectations, standards, opinions, from those members of society who are passing out of the group life to those who are coming into it, social life could not survive. If the members who compose a
45 society lived on continuously, they might educate the new-born members, but it would be a task directed by personal interest rather than social need. Now it is a work of necessity. If a plague carried off the members of a society all at once, it is obvious that the group would be permanently done for. Yet the death of each of
50 its constituent members is as certain as if an epidemic took them all at once. But the graded difference in age, the fact that some are born as some die, makes possible through transmission of ideas and practices the constant reweaving of the social fabric. Yet this renewal is not automatic. Unless pains are taken to see that
55 genuine and thorough transmission takes place, the most civilized group will relapse into barbarism and then into savagery.

The primary purpose of the passage is to

A) argue that we should spend more money on public schools.

B) explain why the author wants to be a teacher.

C) prove that humans would die without education.

D) support the claim that good education is essential for human beings.

Because this is a general question, save it for last. Not only is the blurb a good clue to the main point, but notice that many of the questions revolve around the idea of education. Choice (A) might be something that the author believes, but public schools are never mentioned in the passage. Choice (C) is too extreme, since the passage says that "social life" would die out, not that humans would literally die, and it is hard to "prove" anything in a short passage. Choice (B) is too personal; the author never discusses his own memories or wishes. The correct answer is (D).

2

The author discusses a stone (lines 2–8) in order to explain

A)   the forces necessary to destroy rock.

B)   the difference between living and non-living beings.

C)   why living things cannot be split into pieces.

D)   why living things are easier to crush than stones.

The stone is an example that illustrates something. What does it illustrate? Read three to five lines above (in this case, from the beginning of the passage) to three to five lines below the example, and look for the idea supported by the case of the stone. The answer is in the first line: "The most notable distinction between living and inanimate things is that the former maintain themselves by renewal." Which choice matches this prediction? Choice (B) does.

3

According to the passage, the "necessity of education" (line 28) is based in the fact that humans

A) have mothers and fathers.

B) have larger brains than any other animal.

C) are more advanced than other animals.

D) are mortal.

Reread line 28 in context to see what the passage says. It states that "the primary ineluctable facts of the birth and death of each one of the constituent members in a social group determine the necessity of education." Which choice is the best match to this line? The fact that humans are born and die—that is, they are mortal—explains the necessity of education. So the answer is (D).

4

The word "pains" as used in line 54 most nearly means

A) aches.

B) grievances.

C) measures.

D) challenges.

Cross off the word "pains" in line 54, reread the sentence, and pick your own word to go in the blank. The word that fills the blank must be something like "steps" or "actions." Which choice comes closest in meaning? Choice (C) does.

5

In the last paragraph, the author implies that without a concerted effort to educate the young, humans

A) will become extinct.

B) may return to a more savage lifestyle.

C) would not be as happy as those with education.

D) will become more like stones.

In the very last sentence of the passage, the author claims that "unless pains are taken to see that genuine and thorough transmission takes place, the most civilized group will relapse into barbarism and then into savagery." What choice best matches this line? Choice (B) does.

Paired Questions

You will notice on every passage, there are two or more sets of questions that are paired together. The first question looks and sounds just like a regular question. It may ask about a detail, it may be an inference question, or it may be a main idea question. The second question in the pair will always ask, "Which choice provides the best evidence for the answer to the previous question?" There are two types of paired questions: specific and general.

Specific Paired Questions

The specific paired questions are a fabulous two-for-one deal. If you're following all the steps of the Treasure Hunt (from page 23), you'll find when you get to the "best evidence" question of a specific paired set, you've already answered it. This is because you've already found the best evidence when you carefully read your window and underlined your prediction. Let's take a look at a set.

6

The passage indicates that physical growth:

A) shares a similar process with biological life.

B) is a necessary prerequisite for education.

C) continually renews the customs of the social group.

D) is not sufficient to sustain a group's social life.

7

Which choice provides the best evidence for the answer to the previous question?

A) Lines 26–28 ("The primary . . . education")

B) Lines 32–34 ("Mere physical . . . group")

C) Lines 40–41 ("Society exists . . . life")

D) Lines 44–47 ("If the . . . need")

Start with the first question. This question is very straightforward to answer by itself. All you need to do is find out what the passage says about physical growth. Although there isn't a given line reference, you can still skim through the text looking for the lead words *phyiscal* and *growth*. You'll find the phrase *physically growing up* in the middle of the third paragraph, in the sentence in lines 32–34. The text clearly states that "Mere physical growing up, mere mastery of the bare necessities of subsistence will not suffice to reproduce the life of the group." Underline that line and choose (D) for question 6. Then, because you already have the "best evidence" underlined, when you get to question 7, you've already answered it. Just find your line reference in (B), bubble it in, and move on.

General Paired Sets and Parallel POE

Not all sets of paired questions will be as easy as specific paired sets, but they'll still be approachable. If you have a paired question that is a main idea/general question or a paired question without a clear Line Reference or Lead Word, Parallel POE is a very useful strategy.

Using Parallel POE, you'll be able to work through the questions at the same time! When you find yourself faced with a set of paired questions, you can start with the second question (the "best evidence" question) if (1) you aren't sure where to look for the answer or (2) the first question is a general question about the whole passage. Because the second question in the pair asks which lines provide the *best evidence* for the previous question, you can use those lines to help work through the answers for the previous question. Let's take a look.

8

Based on the passage as a whole, the author most likely agrees that education is

A) a necessary defense against savagery.

B) a self-renewing process.

C) the gap of knowledge between generations of people.

D) a characteristic of all living things.

9

Which choice provides the best evidence for the answer to the previous question?

A) Lines 8–10 ("While the . . . existence")

B) Lines 16–18 ("With the . . . practices")

C) Lines 30–32 ("With the . . . increases")

D) Lines 54–56 ("Unless pains . . . savagery")

When you read question 8, you might have an initial feeling of, "Well, that could be from anywhere in the passage." Sure could. Now you're potentially faced with the *worst* scavenger hunt ever. Instead of wading through the entire passage, though, and trying to find something you think answers the question and then hope it's included in the "best evidence" question, go to the "best evidence" first! This is the Parallel POE strategy.

What's great about Parallel POE is that the original question does not always matter. Think for a moment about how paired questions operate. The correct answer to the first question *must* be supported by an answer to the evidence question, and the correct answer to the evidence question *must* support an answer to the first question. In other words, if there is an evidence answer that doesn't match with an answer to the first question, it is wrong. Period. Likewise, if there is an answer to the first question that isn't supported by an evidence answer, it too is wrong. Period.

Use this to your advantage! Rather than worry about what the first question is asking and what the answer might be, just start making connections between the two answer sets. If an evidence answer supports a first question answer, literally draw a line connecting them. You should not expect to have four connections. If you are lucky, you will have only one connection, and you will therefore have your answer pair. Otherwise, you might have two or three connections and will then (and only then) worry about the first question. The important thing to remember is that any answer choice in the first question that isn't physically connected to an evidence answer—and any evidence answer that isn't connected to an answer in the first question—must be eliminated.

Take a look at how this first Parallel POE pass would look. (The paired questions have been arranged in two columns to help demonstrate this process, and the lines have been written out for your convenience.)

8. Based on the passage as a whole, the author most likely agrees that education is
   A) a necessary defense against savagery.
   B) a self-renewing process.
   C) the gap of knowledge between generations of people.
   D) a characteristic of all living things.

9. Which choice provides the best evidence for the answer to the previous question?
   A) "While the living thing may easily be crushed by superior force, it nonetheless tries to turn the energies that act upon it into means of its own further existence."
   B) "With the renewal of physical existence goes, in the case of human beings, the recreation of beliefs, ideals, hopes, happiness, misery, and practices."
   C) "With the growth of civilization, the gap between the original capacities of the immature and the standards and customs of the elders increases."
   D) "Unless pains are taken to see that genuine and thorough transmission takes place, the most civilized group will relapse into barbarism and then into savagery."

Don't worry about the question itself yet. Go straight to the "best evidence" lines.

- 9 (A) says "the living thing... tries to turn the energies that act upon it into means of its own further existence." Read through all four answer choices for question 8. Do you see any answers that those lines support? Although 8 (D) talks about "living things," it is not a good match to the quote. Plus, it is too extreme (*all*). There's nothing that is supported by these lines, so you can eliminate 9 (A). It doesn't matter what the question asks; if there's no support, the answer cannot be right.

- 9 (B) says "With the renewal of physical existence goes, in the case of human beings, the recreation of beliefs, ideals, hopes, happiness, misery, and practices." Looking through the answers for question 8, there seems to be a connection with the word "renewal" in 8 (B). Just a match of one word doesn't make a great match, however, so don't be fooled by this one. There is likely a much better match between a different pair of answers.

- 9 (C) says "With the growth of civilization, the gap between the original capacities of the immature and the standards and customs of the elders increases." Notice 8 (C) pretty much says the same thing? Draw a line connecting 9 (C) with 8 (C). Nothing else from question 8 matches with 9 (C), so move on to 9 (D).

- 9 (D) says "the most civilized group will relapse into barbarism and then into savagery," which seems to pretty clearly support 8 (A). Draw a line physically connecting 9 (D) with 8 (A).

Now, notice that (B) and (D) in question 8 "have little to no support." Regardless of the question or what you read in the text, if the answers have no support from the "best evidence" question, they cannot be right. Eliminate those two.

Your question should look something like this at this point:

| 8. Based on the passage as a whole, the author most likely agrees that education is
A) a necessary defense against savagery.
B) ~~a self-renewing process.~~
C) the gap of knowledge between generations of people.
D) ~~a characteristic of all living things.~~ | 9. Which choice provides the best evidence for the answer to the previous question?
A) ~~"While the living thing may easily be crushed by superior force, it nonetheless tries to turn the energies that act upon it into means of its own further existence."~~
B) ~~"With the renewal of physical existence goes, in the case of human beings, the recreation of beliefs, ideals, hopes, happiness, misery, and practices."~~
C) "With the growth of civilization, the gap between the original capacities of the immature and the standards and customs of the elders increases."
D) "Unless pains are taken to see that genuine and thorough transmission takes place, the most civilized group will relapse into barbarism and then into savagery." |

Now you're down to a very nice 50/50 split. Go back to the question. Of the two pairs, which one best describes a way the author would view education? The gap of knowledge between generations is the gap education is supposed to fill, not the definition of education itself, so you can eliminate the 8 (C)/9 (C) pair, leaving you with the correct answer of 8 (A)/9 (D).

On the official test, it would be too complicated to draw a full table, so all you need to do is create a column to the left of the "best evidence" choices for the answers to the previous question. It should look something like this:

Q8

9. Which choice provides the best evidence for the answer to the previous question?

A

C   C) Lines 30–32 ("With the ... increases")

D) Lines 54–56 ("Unless pains ... savagery")

Dual Passage

One passage in the Reading Test will be a dual passage, that is, two passages that have differing viewpoints on a common theme. Following the passages will be some questions that are relevant to only one passage or the other and some questions that ask you to compare the two passages. These comparison questions are usually harder, so the best strategy is as follows:

1. Read the blurb to see what the passages are about.

2. Answer the questions for Passage 1.

3. Answer the questions for Passage 2.

4. Answer any questions that ask you to compare the two passages.

This way, you'll save the hardest problems for last—and if you run out of time, you can skip them entirely.

Step 4: Writing and Language

What Grammar Rules Will be Tested?

The grammar tested on the SAT is fairly basic. You won't be expected to know a great number of obscure rules; instead, you'll be expected to know a handful of rules very well. Most of the questions in Writing and Language will test your knowledge of one or more of the following topics:

1. **Verbs**

   Verbs must be in agreement with their subjects, be in the proper tense, be described by adverbs, and be in the same format as other verbs in the sentence.

2. **Pronouns**

   Pronouns must agree with the nouns they replace, be in the proper case, and unambiguously refer to only one specific noun.

3. **Punctuation**

   Periods and semicolons (;) are used to separate two complete thoughts. Commas are used for incomplete thoughts and should be used only when needed. Colons (:) are used to introduce an idea or a list. The information that precedes a colon must be a complete sentence.

4. **Apostrophes**

   Apostrophes are used for only two reasons: to show possession ("Sara's cat") or for contractions ("you're").

5. Transitions

Transitions are used to show the direction of the ideas in the passage. They may appear at the beginning of the sentence to mark a new thought, in the middle of a sentence to connect ideas, or as the entire topic sentence of a paragraph.

6. Commonly Misused Words

They're means *they are. Their* is a possessive pronoun. *There* is used to indicate location.

You're means *you are. Your* is a possessive pronoun.

It's means *it is. Its* is a possessive pronoun.

In addition to the problems above, also remember the three Cs:
- **Clear**—The meaning of the sentence must always be as clear as possible.
- **Consistent**—Keep words and phrases as consistent as possible.
- **Concise**—In many cases (not all), shorter answers are better than longer answers.

What Kinds of Questions Are on This Test?

"Proofreader" questions—Short and specific, these require no more than one or two sentences of context within the passage.

"Editor" questions—These require knowledge of the broader organization of the passage (or paragraph).

Over the next few pages, we'll discuss a general strategy for each question type. Then we will go into more detail about the specific grammar rules that will be tested.

How to Approach Proofreader Questions

Here's a sample proofreader question:

The history of **1** language although it may sound like a boring subject, is a treasure trove of historical, cultural, and psychological insights.

A) NO CHANGE

B) language, although it may sound like a boring subject

C) language, although it may sound, like a boring subject,

D) language, although it may sound like a boring subject,

Most students make the mistake of reading the sentence four times, with each of the answers substituted in, to figure out what *sounds* right. However, this is not a very safe or efficient way of tackling these problems. Notice how all of the answers are virtually identical. The ONLY difference is in the placement of commas. So, rather than reading the sentence over and over again, just go straight to the answers! Ask yourself "what's changing?" and then use POE to find the right answer. (In case you're curious, the answer is (D). We'll get to the reason for that a bit later.) Let's try another:

Language is a living **2** document shows how people think and communicate.

2

A) NO CHANGE

B) document it shows

C) document that shows

D) document, which showing

First, look at what's changing in the answer choices. The word "document" remains the same in each, but what comes after it changes each time. This question, then, seems to be asking, "Which words will best link the two ideas in the sentence?"

Choices (A) and (D) make the sentence incomplete, so those should be eliminated.

Choice (B) connects two complete sentences with no punctuation, so that should also be eliminated.

It looks like only (C) appropriately links the ideas without adding new errors.

Notice how that entire process started with the question, "What's changing in the answer choices?" With that question you can determine what the question is testing and use POE to do the rest.

> **3** Additionally, this does
> not tell the whole story.

3
A) NO CHANGE
B) However,
C) Therefore,
D) As a result,

Here, the answer to "what's changing in the answer choices?" is "transitions." Even if you don't have the rest of the passage to work with, you may notice that "additionally," "therefore," and "as a result" can all be used to join similar ideas. Because these all go in the same directions, it is unlikely that one will be better than the others. Only "however" shows the contrast that is needed if we aren't getting "the whole story." Although transitions are not always as simple as "same direction" or "opposite direction," thinking about how to properly join the ideas is the key to answering these questions.

Let's try another.

A community's very soul, we might say, is communicated through ▮4▮ their language.

4

A) NO CHANGE

B) they're language.

C) their languages.

D) its language.

As always, start with what is changing in the answer choices. It looks like the main change is between the words "they're," "their," and "its," with a minor change between the words "language" and "languages." As such, this question seems to be asking, "What is the appropriate pronoun to use in this context, and just how many "languages" are we talking about?"

Start wherever is easiest. In this case, it can be a little bit difficult to say for sure whether the question is talking about one language or a bunch of languages. Instead, work with the pronoun. What does it refer to? In this sentence, the pronoun refers to "a community," which is a singular noun (even though it describes a lot of people). Therefore, the only possible answer is (D), which contains the singular pronoun "its."

Notice how you never needed to determine whether it should be language or languages.

Sometimes fixing one problem will make others irrelevant!

Your Turn—Exercise 4.1

Although the military knows how to construct tires that do not need replacing, they cannot sell them publicly for fear of collapsing the tire industry.

1

A) NO CHANGE

B) which do not need replacing; they cannot sell them publicly for

C) that do not need replacing, it cannot sell them publicly for

D) that do not need replacing: it cannot sell them publicly in

The all-star team, composed of girls from small, rural schools scattered throughout the state and the first such team **2** to beat competitors from larger schools, were sad to see the tournament come to an end.

2

A) NO CHANGE

B) which beats competitors from larger schools, were sad to see the tournament come

C) to beat competitors from larger schools, was sad to see the tournament come

D) to beat competitor's from larger schools, were sad to see the tournament came

The study revealed that in families in which parents were involved in their children's education, children **3** will learn to read more easily, whereas when parents focused on their own work, children tended to struggle in the most basic subjects.

3

A) NO CHANGE
B) learned
C) are learning
D) learning

Sarah has great regard for Napoleon Bonaparte, **4** whom she considers a brilliant military strategist, despite the debacle at Waterloo.

4

A) NO CHANGE
B) who
C) that
D) which

The stage manager said that even if the theatre were **5** ten times bigger she still would not have enough space to give each member of the cast their own dressing room.

5

A) NO CHANGE
B) ten times bigger she still would not have enough space to give each member of the cast they're
C) ten times bigger she still would not have enough space to give each member of the cast there
D) ten times bigger she still would not have enough space to give each member of the cast his or her

Answers and Explanations to Exercise 4.1

1. **C** One of the issues here is pronoun consistency. The plural word "they" cannot refer to the singular word "military." As for punctuation, the beginning of the sentence is not a complete thought, so rule out anything except a comma after "replacing."

2. **C** Always check that verbs are consistent with their subjects. The subject of the sentence, "team," is singular, while the verb, "were," is plural. Choice (D) is also wrong because of the use of an apostrophe (the "competitors" do not possess anything).

3. **B** The sentence is in the past tense, as indicated by "revealed" and "focused." Choice (A), "will learn," is in the future tense, which does not make sense in the context of the sentence. Choices (C) and (D) are present tense. Choice (B) is the only past tense verb.

4. **A** Since Napoleon Bonaparte is a person, you need either "who" or "whom." "Who" is used similarly to "he," "she," or "they." "Whom" is used similarly to "him," "her," or "them." She considers "him" a brilliant military strategist, so keep the sentence as it is written.

5. **D** Always check pronouns for consistency with the nouns they replace. The pronoun "their" (plural) refers to the noun "member" (singular). Eliminate (A). "They're" means "they are" and does not fit. "There" refers to location.

How to Approach Editor Questions

Editor questions sometimes test the same types of rules found in the proofreader questions. In other cases, editor questions are entirely about the structure of ideas in a paragraph or the entire passage. Luckily, using Process of Elimination is an effective tool on these kinds of questions.

Try this one:

The problem has certainly gained a good deal of traction in public debates. The fact that it has gained such traction makes us wonder why isn't there more significant action to combat the gender pay gap. █1█

█1█

Which of the following gives the best way to combine these two sentences?

A) The problem has certainly gained a good deal of traction in public debates; the fact that it has gained such traction makes us wonder why isn't there more significant action to combat the gender pay gap.

B) The problem has certainly gained a good deal of traction in public debates, which raises the question of why more isn't being done to combat the gap.

C) The problem has certainly gained a good deal of traction in public debates: this fact of more public attention raises a serious question of why more isn't being done to close that gap.

D) The problem has certainly gained a good deal of traction in public debates. Why isn't more being done to combat the gap?

The question asks us to combine the two sentences. Your eyes were probably drawn immediately to (D), which is the most concise of the choices. There's just one problem: (D) doesn't answer the question! The question asks to combine the sentences, and while (D) shortens them, it doesn't combine them.

Choice (B) is, therefore, the best option. It combines the sentences and shortens them a bit, unlike (A) and (C), which combine the sentences but don't really do much beyond changing the punctuation. On combination questions, make sure you are choosing the answer that eliminates repetitive phrases and has the appropriate transition between parts.

Here is a type of question that shows up on every test:

The question of unequal pay for women draws on many other broader social issues.

The writer is considering deleting the phrase "of unequal pay for women" from the preceding sentence. Should this phrase be kept or deleted?

A) Kept, because removing it would remove a crucial piece of information from this part of the sentence.

B) Kept, because it reminds the reader of social injustice in the modern world.

C) Deleted, because it wrongly implies that there is a disparity between what women and men are paid.

D) Deleted, because it gives information that has no bearing on this particular text.

This question asks whether you should keep or delete the phrase "of unequal pay for women." Without that phrase, the sentence reads, "The question draws on many other broader social issues." Because nothing in this sentence or any of the previous ones specifies what this "question" might be, you should keep the phrase. You want to be as precise as possible!

And, as (A) says, you want to keep the phrase because it is crucial to clarifying precisely what "the question" is. Choice (B) is a little too grandiose a reason to keep the phrase, especially when the whole passage (as you will soon see) is about the particular injustice of the gender pay gap. Choice (A) is, therefore, the best answer.

Here is another staple of the Writing and Language Test:

The gender disparities persist in areas other than pay. Women have only had the right to vote since 1920, when the 19th amendment was ratified. **3** There is a long history of misogyny written into the very cultural and social fabric of the United States.

 3

At the point, the writer is considering adding the following true statement:

> The year that women's suffrage became legal in the United States was also the year that the American Football League was formed under the leadership of Jim Thorpe.

Should the writer make this addition here?

A) Yes, because it gives a broader context to the achievement of women's suffrage.

B) Yes, because it helps to ease some of the political rhetoric in the rest of the passage.

C) No, because it does not contribute in a significant way to the discussion of the gender pay gap.

D) No, because the question of gender pay is irrelevant when all football players are men.

The proposed sentence does contain an interesting bit of information, but that piece of information has no clear place either in these few sentences or in the passage as a whole. Therefore, it should not be added, thus eliminating (A) and (B).

Then, because it does not play a significant role in the passage, the sentence should not be added for the reason stated in (C). While (D) may be true in a way, it does not reflect anything clearly relating to the role the sentence might play in the passage as a whole. Read literally, and answer as literally and precisely as you can.

Now that you know how to approach both Proofreader and Editor questions, let's take a closer look at some of the specific grammar issues that you will be sure to see in Writing and Language questions, as well as ways those issues will be tested.

Punctuation

STOP
- Period
- Semicolon
- Comma + FANBOYS
- Question mark
- Exclamation mark

HALF-STOP
- Colon
- Long dash

GO
- Comma
- No punctuation

> **FANBOYS** stands for the conjunctions **F**or, **A**nd, **N**or, **B**ut, **O**r, **Y**et, and **S**o.

STOP punctuation can link _only_ complete ideas.

HALF-STOP punctuation must be _preceded_ by a complete idea.

GO punctuation can link anything _except_ two complete ideas.

What's a "complete idea," you may ask? It is an idea that can stand on its own and will make sense to the reader. At minimum, a sentence must have a subject and a verb to be complete (as in, "I swam.").

Jonah studied every day for
the big **1** test he was taking the
SAT that Saturday.

A) NO CHANGE

B) test, he was taking

C) test he was taking,

D) test; he was taking

As always, check what's changing in the answer choices. In this case, the words all stay the same. Only the punctuation is changing. Specifically, notice the type of punctuation changing: STOP and GO.

Now, when you see STOP punctuation changing in the answer choices, you can do a little something called the Vertical Line Test.

In the sentence next to the question, draw a line where you see the punctuation changing—in this case, between the words "test" and "he." Then, read up to the vertical line: "Jonah studied every day for the big test." That's complete. Now, read after the vertical line: "he was taking the SAT that Saturday." That's also complete.

So think for a minute; you have two complete ideas here. What kind of punctuation do you need? STOP or HALF-STOP. It looks like STOP is the only one available, so choose (D).

Let's try another.

It was very important for
him to do **2** well. High scores
in all the subjects.

A) NO CHANGE

B) well; high

C) well: high

D) well, he wanted high

Check the answer choices. What's changing? It looks like the punctuation is changing, and some of that punctuation is STOP. Use the Vertical Line Test. Draw a vertical line where you see the punctuation: between "well" and "high" in the original sentence.

What's before the vertical line? "It was very important for him to do well" is complete. Then, "high scores in all the subjects" is not. Therefore, because you have one complete idea (the first) and one incomplete idea (the second), you can't use STOP punctuation, thus eliminating (A) and (B). Note that these answers are basically the same, so they can both be eliminated no matter what the passage says.

Now, what's different between the last two? Choice (C) contains HALF-STOP punctuation, which can work, so keep that. Choice (D) adds some words, with which the second idea becomes "he wanted high scores in all the subjects," which is complete. That makes two complete ideas separated by a comma, but this would require STOP punctuation! Eliminate (D). Only (C) is left.

Let's see one more.

Whenever Jonah had a free

3 moment—he was studying.

3

A) NO CHANGE

B) moment; he

C) moment, he,

D) moment, he

The punctuation is changing in the answer choices, and there's some STOP punctuation. Use the Vertical Line Test. Put the line between "moment" and "he." The first idea, "Whenever Jonah had a free moment," is incomplete, and the second idea, "he was studying," is complete. Therefore, you can't use STOP (which needs two complete ideas) or HALF-STOP (which needs a complete idea before the punctuation), thus eliminating (A) and (B). Then, because there is no good reason to put a comma after the word "he," the correct answer must be (D).

Commas

If you can't cite a reason to use a comma, *don't use one*.

On the SAT, there are only four reasons to use a comma:
- in STOP punctuation with one of the FANBOYS
- in GO punctuation to separate incomplete ideas from other ideas
- in a list of three or more things
- in a sentence containing unnecessary information

You've already seen the first two concepts, so let's look at the other two.

Try this one.

His top-choice schools were

4 Harvard, Yale and Princeton.

| 4 |

A) NO CHANGE

B) Harvard, Yale, and Princeton.

C) Harvard, Yale, and, Princeton.

D) Harvard Yale and Princeton.

First, check what's changing in the answer choices. The commas in this list are changing. Because there's not any obvious STOP or HALF-STOP punctuation, the Vertical Line Test won't help on this one.

However, it does help to know that the SAT wants a comma after every item in a series. Think of it this way. There's a potential misunderstanding in this sentence:

"I went to the park with my parents, my cat Violet and my dog Stuart."

Without a comma, it sure sounds like the cat and the dog are the speaker's parents. When there is no comma in the list, there is no way to tell whether the cat and the dog are the parents, or if they are additional members of the family that went to the park. The only way to remove the ambiguity would be to add a comma like this:

"I went to the park with my parents, my cat Violet, and my dog Stuart."

Now look back at question 4 above. In this problem, "Harvard, Yale, and Princeton" form a list, so they should be set off by commas as they are in (B). Be careful of (C), which adds an additional, unnecessary comma after "and."

Let's try another.

5 Jonah, everyone seemed fairly certain, was going to get into one of those schools.

5

A) NO CHANGE

B) Jonah everyone seemed fairly certain

C) Jonah, everyone seemed fairly certain

D) Jonah everyone seemed fairly certain,

First, check what's changing in the answer choices. Just commas. And those commas seem to be circling around the words "everyone seemed fairly certain." When you've got a few commas circling around a word, phrase, or clause, the question is usually testing necessary vs. unnecessary information. Unnecessary information should have a comma both before and after it.

A good way to test whether the idea is necessary to the meaning of the sentence is to take it out. Read the original sentence again. Now read this one: "Jonah was going to get into one of those schools."

Is the sentence still complete? Yes. Has the meaning of the sentence changed? No, you just lost a little extra detail. Therefore, the idea is *unnecessary* to the meaning of the sentence and should be set off with commas both before and after it as it is in (A).

Apostrophes

As with commas, if you can't cite a reason to use an apostrophe, don't use one. There are only two reasons to use apostrophes on the SAT:
- Possessive nouns (NOT pronouns)
- Contractions

Take a look at some examples.

Some of those very **6**
selective schools' require really high score's.

6

A) NO CHANGE
B) selective school's require really high scores'.
C) selective schools require really high score's.
D) selective schools require really high scores.

Check what's changing in the answer choices. In this case, the words all remain the same, but the apostrophes are changing. Remember: you don't want to use apostrophes at all if you can't cite a good reason to do so.

Does anything belong to "schools" or "score"? No! Are they forming contractions like "school is" or "score is"? No! Therefore, there's no reason to use apostrophes, and the only possible answer is (D), which dispenses with the apostrophes altogether.

The question was testing whether you can spot unnecessary punctuation.

But sometimes the apostrophes will be necessary. Have a look at another.

7 It's tough to get in to
you're top-choice schools.

 7

A) NO CHANGE

B) Its tough to get in to your

C) Its tough to get in to
you're

D) It's tough to get in to your

Check what's changing in the answer choices. The main changes have to do with apostrophes, particularly on the words "its/it's" and "your/you're."

The first word, "its/it's," needs an apostrophe: it creates the contraction "it is." Therefore, because this one needs an apostrophe, get rid of (B) and (C). As for the "your/you're," this word is possessive (as in, the "top-choice schools" belonging to "you"). Remember that possessive *nouns* need an apostrophe, but possessive *pronouns* don't. Therefore, because "you" is a pronoun, this word should be spelled "your," as it is in (D).

Verb Consistency

The speakers of what has come to be known as Appalachian English has used a form of English that few can explain.

1

A) NO CHANGE

B) Appalachian English uses

C) Appalachian English use

D) Appalachian English using

First, as always, check what's changing in the answer choices. In this case, "Appalachian English" stays the same, but the forms of the verb *to use* change. Therefore, because the verbs change, you know that the question is testing verbs.

When you see verbs changing in the answer choices, the first thing to check is the subject of the sentence. Is the verb consistent with the subject? In this case, it's not. The subject of this sentence is "speakers," which is plural. Therefore, eliminate (A) and (B). Since (D) creates an incomplete idea, only (C) can work in the context.

Anytime you see verbs changing in the answer choices, check the subject first. Subjects and verbs need to be consistent with each other. Often, the subject will be separated from the verb by a few words or phrases, so be careful!

Take a look at another.

Many scholars believe
Appalachian pronunciation comes
from Scots-Irish immigration,
but some 2 theorizes that this
dialect of English may be closer
to what Londoners spoke in
Elizabethan times.

2

A) NO CHANGE
B) theorized
C) have theorized
D) theorize

Check what's changing in the answer choices: it's the verbs. Remember from the first question that when you see verbs changing, make sure the verb is consistent with the subject. Because the subject of this sentence is "some," which is plural, you can eliminate (A), which isn't consistent.

Then, because all the others are consistent with the subject, make sure they are consistent with the other verbs. All the other verbs in this sentence—"believe, comes, may be"—are in the present tense, so the underlined verb should be as well, as it is in (D). Choices (B) and (C) could work in some contexts but not this one!

As you can see, verbs are all about consistency.

Bad Comparisons

Aside from verbs, consistency can show up in other ways as well. Take a look this question.

The language of the West Virginians in Applachia is almost nothing like **3** New Yorkers or even other West Virginians.

3

A) NO CHANGE

B) the language of New Yorker's or even other West Virginian's.

C) that of New Yorkers or even other West Virginians.

D) people from New York or from West Virginia.

Look at what's changing in the answer choices. The main change is between the nouns—"New Yorkers or even other West Virginians" and "the language." You saw in the last question that when nouns are changing in the answer choices you need to make sure those nouns are consistent with other nouns in the sentence.

In this case, the nouns are being compared. The intent is to compare the language of Appalachia with the language of New Yorkers and West Virginians. Choices (A) and (D) suggest that the "language" is being compared with the "people," so these are inconsistent. Then, (B) contains some unnecessary apostrophes, so only (C) is left.

Nouns have to be consistent with other nouns. When the answer choices show a change in nouns, look for the sentence's other nouns. They'll provide the clue!

Scholars today are not sure whether to call it a purely European dialect or [4] a uniquely American one.

4

A) NO CHANGE

B) uniquely American.

C) a unique one.

D) American.

Check what's changing in the answer choices. There's a fairly significant change between "American" and "American one." The part of the sentence right before the underlined portion refers to a "European dialect," so you should make the sentence consistent: an "American dialect," not merely "American," as in (B) and (D).

Then, you are down to (A) and (C). The difference here comes between the words "unique" and "uniquely American." While you do want to be concise when possible, you need to make sure first and foremost that you are being *precise*. Choice (A) is more precise than (C) in that it has a clearer relation to the "European dialect" with which it is being contrasted. Therefore, (A) is the best answer because it is the most *consistent* with the rest of the sentence and the most *precise* of the remaining possible answers.

Clarity

Consistency is probably the most important thing on the SAT, but clarity is a close second. Once you've made sure that the underlined portion is consistent with the rest of the sentence, then make sure that the underlined portion is as clear as possible. Perfect grammar is one thing, but it won't matter much if no one knows what the writer is talking about!

Really, **5** most are collections of many influences, but the Appalachian dialect seems unique.

5

A) NO CHANGE

B) most of them

C) most Americans

D) most American dialects

Check what's changing in the answer choices. The changes could be summed up with the question "*most* what?" You have four different options, so use your main guiding principles of consistency and precision.

First of all, there's a comparison in this sentence between different kinds of "dialects," so (C) can be eliminated because that explicitly changes the comparison to something that is inconsistent.

Then, be as precise as possible. Choices (A) and (B) are very similar in that they say "most," but they don't specify *what* that "most" refers to. Even though these are grammatically consistent with the rest of the sentence, they're not quite precise enough, which makes (D) a lot better.

Take a look at this question.

The Appalachian region's
[6] isolation has led to some
hypotheses from major urban
centers that its dialect has
remained intact from the days of
its earliest settlers.

 6

A) NO CHANGE

B) isolation has led to some hypotheses that its dialect from major urban centers has remained intact

C) isolation from major urban centers has led to some hypotheses that its dialect has remained intact

D) isolation has led to some hypotheses that its dialect has remained intact from major urban centers

Check what's changing in the answer choices. This step is crucial here because there are no obvious grammatical errors, so the answer choices are essential to figuring out exactly what the question is asking you to do.

The only difference among the answer choices is that the phrase "from major urban centers" is in different places. In the end, you will just need to put that phrase in the most precise place, hopefully right next to whatever it is modifying.

In this case, you can choose from among "hypotheses," "dialect," "isolation," and "intact." Which of these would have the most precise need for the phrase "from major urban centers"? Because "urban centers" is associated with place, you should eliminate (A), "hypotheses," and (D), "intact," which don't have anything to do with place. Then, because the passage as a whole has talked about the remoteness of the Appalachian dialect, you can say for sure that it is not a "dialect from major urban centers," eliminating (B). All that remains, then, is (C), which completes the phrase "isolation from major urban centers" and is the most precise answer possible.

Misplaced Modifiers

The last question tested a topic called "misplaced modifiers." Modifiers are descriptive phrases in a sentence; misplaced modifiers are in the wrong place in the sentence. Often, they appear at the beginning of the sentence, set off with a comma. No matter where they are, check to see what noun is placed next to the modifying phrase.

Signed in Mexico City on February 2, 1848, the boundaries of the United States were extended by The Treaty of Guadalupe Hidalgo.

7

A) NO CHANGE

B) the United States boundaries were extended by the Treaty of Guadalupe Hidalgo

C) the United States extended its boundaries by the Treaty of Guadalupe Hidalgo

D) the Treaty of Guadalupe Hidalgo extended the boundaries of the United States

In this sentence, the modifying phrase is "Signed in Mexico City on February 2, 1848." However, the noun directly following it is "the boundaries of the United States." Clearly, the boundaries weren't signed in 1848. Eliminate (A), (B), and (C). The best answer is (D). (Give yourself a big bonus if you noticed the lack of an apostrophe after "United States" in answer (B).)

Try one more.

Although the meals at
Eli's Saucy Seafood were tasty,
8 Ron's Bulkhead was an
outstanding restaurant.

8

A) NO CHANGE

B) Ron's Bulkhead is much better.

C) the entrees at Ron's Bulkhead were infinitely better.

D) Ron's Bulkhead is an outstanding restaurant.

This one combines a bad comparison with a misplaced modifier. Choice (C) correctly compares the meals at Eli's with the meals at Ron's. Choices (A), (B), and (D) incorrectly compare the meals at Eli's with various characteristics of Ron's Bulkhead, not the meals themselves and therefore can be eliminated.

Concision

If you were to ask for directions, which answer would you rather receive?

Turn right at Main Street and walk four blocks.

or

Since this street, Elm Street, is facing in a northerly direction, and your destination is due northeast, go east when you arrive at the intersection of Elm and Main. Going east will entail making a right turn in quite that easterly direction. After having made this turn and arrived on the perpendicular street...

The first one, obviously.

And that's because concision is key when you want to communicate meaning. Really, as long as everything else is in order—as long as the grammar and punctuation are good to go and the sentence is clear and precise—the best answer will almost always be the shortest.

Take a look at an example.

It is precisely this isolation that has led many scholars to believe that Appalachian English is **9** alike and similar to the English spoken in Shakespeare's time.

9
A) NO CHANGE
B) similar
C) likely similar
D) similarly alike

Check what's changing in the answer choices. In this case, the word "similar" appears in all the answer choices, and in some it is paired with the word "alike." Typically, if you see a list of answer choices wherein one answer is short and the rest mean the same thing but are longer, the question is testing concision.

What, after all, is the difference between the words "similar" and "alike"? There really isn't one, so there's no use in saying both of them, as in (A), or pairing them awkwardly, as in (D). In fact, the shortest answer, (B), does everything the other choices do, but it does so in the fewest words. Choice (B) is therefore the correct answer.

Try one more.

10 Whatever the case may be, the Appalachian dialect is fascinating, and we can only hope that it persists against the onslaught of mass media.

10

A) NO CHANGE

B) Whoop-de-doo, the Appalachian dialect

C) All things considered, the Appalachian dialect

D) The Appalachian dialect

As always, check what's changing in the answer choices. The changes could be summed up like this: There's a bunch of stuff before the phrase "the Appalachian dialect." Does any of that stuff contribute in a significant way to the sentence? No. Does the phrase "the Appalachian dialect" alone help the sentence to fulfill its basic purpose? Yes. Therefore, the best answer is (D).

As you have seen in this chapter, when the SAT is testing *words* (any time the words are changing in the answer choices), make sure that those words are

- **Consistent.** Verbs, nouns, and pronouns should agree within sentences and passages.

- **Clear and precise.** The writing should communicate specific ideas and events.

- **Concise.** When everything else is correct and precise, the shortest answer is the best.

Your Turn—Exercise 4.2

War and Peace (1869) is
1 well-known and famous
mainly for its length. Not many
readers, especially in the modern
day, **2** has the time or the
patience to work through Leo
Tolstoy's 1,400 pages, countless
characters, and plot twists.
3 They are missing a major
opportunity, not only because the
novel is more fun than its page
count suggests, but also because
it marks the end of a particular
moment in history.

1

A) NO CHANGE
B) famous and well-known
C) famously well-known
D) well-known

2

A) NO CHANGE
B) have
C) are having
D) do have

3

A) NO CHANGE
B) Those readers
C) Many of them
D) Some

Czech novelist Milan Kundera cited Tolstoy as the last novelist who could 4 be possessing the sum of his era's human knowledge. This may seem like an odd claim. Some people may be very intelligent, others may be know-it-alls, but is it really possible to know everything? A book like *War and Peace* makes the case that it is possible to know it all, or at least that it *was* possible, 5 alongside Tolstoy's other great novels and non-fiction writings.

4

A) NO CHANGE
B) of had
C) possess
D) possessed

5

If the punctuation were adjusted accordingly, the best placement for the underlined portion would be

A) where it is now.
B) at the beginning of the sentence.
C) after the word "that."
D) after the word "least."

Shakespeare **6** seemed to have an emotional vocabulary that was advanced for his age, but Tolstoy lived in **7** an era of facts and discoveries, and his novels show the fruits of his vast study. It is frankly conceivable that a man with Tolstoy's leisure, intelligence, and curiosity **8** learns about his age's most current findings in literature, politics, religion, and science.

6

A) NO CHANGE
B) seems having
C) has
D) seemingly has

7

A) NO CHANGE
B) an era,
C) a historical time period,
D) one,

8

A) NO CHANGE
B) had been learning
C) could have learned
D) are learning

The very fact that such an achievement is impossible now shows us just how much things have changed since Tolstoy's death in 1910. **9** This was the year, in fact, that Virginia Woolf cited in her oft-quoted remark, "On or about 1910 human character changed." If we at least entertain the idea that she is correct, we can begin to see why she would be willing to make such a grandiose remark. After 1910, the twentieth century started in earnest. Knowledge became more complex as it became more specialized, and although airplanes seemed to make the world a smaller place, the differences among all the places in that small world truly emerged.

9

The writer is considering deleting the phrase "since Tolstoy's death in 1910" and ending the sentence with a period after the word "changed." Should the phrase be kept or deleted?

A) Kept, because it contributes to the essay's biographical sketch of the author of *War and Peace.*

B) Kept, because it introduces a topic of discussion that is continued throughout the paragraph.

C) Deleted, because the remainder of the paragraph describes the insignificance of Tolstoy's death.

D) Deleted, because the paragraph as a whole is focused on the achievements of another author.

War and Peace is the great document of that pre-1910 era, of a moment when the great scientists were also **10** into philosophy and when the great mathematicians were also the great theologians. A great discovery in one field could also be **11** another. Although it was certainly remarkable, it was also possible for a man like Tolstoy to have a fundamental grasp of all that united the many branches of knowledge. Tolstoy's achievement is impossible today, but it is a wonderful reminder of the value of intellectual curiosity and cosmopolitanism. No matter how brilliant and refined we may become, we can always stand to be reminded that there is a world outside of our immediate circle.

10

A) NO CHANGE
B) fascinated with philosophical inquiry
C) interested in philosophy
D) the great philosophers

11

A) NO CHANGE
B) another field.
C) a great discovery for another.
D) the same thing elsewhere.

Answers to Exercise 4.2

1. **D** The answer choices have the words "famous" and "well-known," which are synonyms, so they don't both need to be said. Eliminate (A), (B), and (C). Choice (D) is concise and clear, so it's the correct answer.

2. **B** Verbs change in the answers. The subject is "readers," which is plural. Eliminate (A) because it's singular. The remaining options are all plural and present tense. Choice (B) is concise and works in the sentence, so eliminate (C) and (D) because they add words unnecessarily.

3. **B** Pronouns and nouns change in the answers. The words "they," "them," and "some" are all vague. Choice (B) is clear, so it's the correct answer. Remember that clarity comes before being concise.

4. **C** Verbs change in the answers. The phrase "could of" is never correct (it's "could have" or "could've"), so eliminate (B). "Could possessed" doesn't work because a present tense verb needs to follow "could," so eliminate (D). Choice (A) is more awkwardly phrased than (C), and (C) is more concise, so it's the correct answer.

5. **B** The previous two sentences discuss Tolstoy but not any specific books. Thus, it makes sense for the phrase to go at the beginning of the sentence to transition from Tolstoy to his books to one particular book. Also, the underlined portion draws a comparison, so the thing it's comparing to ("a book like *War and Peace*") should come directly after.

6. **A** Verb tense changes in the answer choices. The sentence discusses Shakespeare and uses the past tense verb "was advanced," so this verb should be in past tense. Only (A) is in past tense.

7. **A** The length of the answer choices changes, so consider whether more words are needed. Choice (D) is the shortest option, but it's not clear what "one" would refer to, so it's incorrect. Choice (B) is the next shortest, but to say

"Tolstoy lived in an era" is not a very meaningful idea. The same is true for (C). Choice (A) provides information about the era or time period that relates to what is stated later in the sentence, so the additional information is needed here.

8. **C** Verb tense changes in the answer choices. The main idea of the sentence is that something is "conceivable," meaning it can be imagined or guessed about. Because of that, the phrase "could have learned" makes the most sense—when you are conceiving of something, it's what "could" happen or have happened, not something that did happen in the past.

9. **B** Try reading the sentence without the phrase: "The very fact that such an achievement is impossible now shows us just how much things have changed." This statement is a little vague because it doesn't explain what the change is or when it occurred. Also, the next sentence says, "This was the year," so this sentence needs to include the year for the second sentence to refer to. Eliminate (C) and (D) because the phrase should be kept. Eliminate (A) because it doesn't contribute to the discussion of Tolstoy so much as it provides context for the other topics in the paragraph.

10. **D** The answers contain similar ideas but are worded differently. The non-underlined portion says, "and when the great mathematicians were also the great theologians." Thus, this part needs to be written in the same form. Choice (D) is in the same form as this phrase.

11. **C** The answer choices have different degrees of specificity. Choice (A) is very vague and makes the sentence confusing. Choice (B) also doesn't make sense—"A great discovery in one field could also be another field." Choice (D) is also vague. Choice (C) is specific and makes the sentence make sense. Even though it repeats some of the same words, this is necessary to provide the meaning that is lacking in the other options.

Grammar Summary

1. Keep your eyes open for the most common types of errors. Make sure you know what types of errors can occur with verbs, pronouns, punctuation, and apostrophes.

2. Checking the changes in the answer choices will let you know which of those errors a question is testing.

3. Make aggressive use of Process of Elimination. Even if you are not sure what the right answer is, eliminate any choices that you know to be wrong and take a guess.

Math
Strategies

Step 5: Plugging In

Imagine you are asked the following two questions:

1. If you have 2 hours to take a test with 3 questions and each question takes you 30 minutes, how much time is remaining when you finish the last question?

2. If you have x hours to take a test with y questions that take you $3z$ minutes each, how much time is remaining when you finish the last question?

The first question should seem much easier. If you try to write an equation for the second one, you have to remember to convert hours to minutes and figure out what to do with the 3. It's easy to make a mistake. It's often much easier to do math with real numbers instead of variables.

You can plug in your own number in place of variables in the questions and answers on a variety of problems on the SAT—like the one in the second question. Just pick a number for the variable (or variables) in a problem, solve the problem using that real number, and then check the answers to see which one matches the correct answer.

Take a look at the following question.

12

Katie and Beth go to lunch together. Katie orders a meal that costs d dollars and Beth orders a meal that costs $3 more than Katie's meal. If 10% sales tax is applied to the total bill, and they split the bill evenly, then how much, in dollars, does each person pay?

A) $2.2d + 3.3$

B) $1.1d + 1.65$

C) $0.55d + 1.65$

D) $0.5d + 1.5$

There are variables in the answer choices, so you can use Plugging In! Start by picking a real number for d. Make $d = \$4$. If Beth's meal is $3 more than Katie's meal, then Beth's meal is $7. Together the meals cost $11. If they split that amount equally, then each girl's bill would be $5.50 before tax. 10% of $5.50 is $0.55, so each girl would pay $5.50 + $0.55 = $6.05. Circle this number on your paper: This is your target answer. Plug in $d = 4$ in the answer choices and see which answer equals your target, $6.05:

A) $2.2(4) + 3.3 = \$8.80 + \$3.30$ Too high! Eliminate (A).

B) $1.1(4) + 1.65 = \$4.40 + \$1.65 = \$6.05$ This matches your target. Keep (B).

C) $0.55(4) + 1.65 = \$2.20 + \$1.65$ Too low! Eliminate (C).

D) $0.5(4) + 1.5 = \$2.00 + \$1.50$ Too low! Eliminate (D)

Only (B) works, so this is your answer!

Plugging In is not just for word problems. It can be especially helpful on some of the tricky algebra questions.

Take a look at this question:

15

The expression $\dfrac{3x - 5}{x + 2}$ is equivalent to which of the following?

A) $3 - \dfrac{5}{2}$

B) $3x - \dfrac{5}{x + 2}$

C) $3 - \dfrac{5}{x + 2}$

D) $3 - \dfrac{11}{x + 2}$

You have a variable in the answer choices, so you can use Plug In. Make $x = 2$. Now the equation becomes $\dfrac{3(2) - 5}{2 + 2}$, which gives you $\dfrac{6 - 5}{4} = \dfrac{1}{4}$. Circle the target of $\dfrac{1}{4}$. Now plug $x = 2$ into each of the answer choices on the following page.

A) $3 - \dfrac{5}{2}$ $= \dfrac{6}{2} - \dfrac{5}{2} = \dfrac{1}{2} \neq \dfrac{1}{4}$

B) $3x - \dfrac{5}{x+2}$ $= 3(2) - \dfrac{5}{2+2} = 6 - \dfrac{5}{4} \neq \dfrac{1}{4}$

C) $3 - \dfrac{5}{x+2}$ $= 3 - \dfrac{5}{2+2} = 3 - \dfrac{5}{4} \neq \dfrac{1}{4}$

D) $3 - \dfrac{11}{x+2}$ $= 3 - \dfrac{11}{2+2} = 3 - \dfrac{11}{4} = \dfrac{12}{4} - \dfrac{11}{4} = \dfrac{1}{4}$

Only (D) gives you the target value of $\dfrac{1}{4}$, so (D) is the correct answer.

Try one more:

10

For $x > 0$, which of the following is

equivalent to $\dfrac{2}{\dfrac{1}{3x} - \dfrac{1}{x-1}}$?

A) $\dfrac{-2x - 1}{6x^2 - 6x}$

B) $\dfrac{6x^2 - 6x}{-2x - 1}$

C) $\dfrac{3x^2 - 3x}{-4x - 2}$

D) $\dfrac{2}{2x + 1}$

If you plug in 2 for x, you will get $\dfrac{2}{\dfrac{1}{6} - \dfrac{1}{1}} = \dfrac{2}{\dfrac{1}{6} - \dfrac{6}{6}} = \dfrac{2}{-\dfrac{5}{6}} = -\dfrac{12}{5}$.

This is your target answer. Substitute $x = 2$ into the answer choices.

Choice (A) becomes $\dfrac{-4 - 1}{6(4) - 6(2)} = -\dfrac{5}{12}$. Eliminate (A). You may

notice though that (B) is the reciprocal of (A) and is therefore $-\dfrac{12}{5}$.

Keep this one, but check the other answers just in case. Choice (C)

is $\dfrac{3(4) - 3(2)}{-8 - 2} = -\dfrac{6}{10}$ and (D) is a positive value. Eliminate (C) and

(D). The answer is (B).

Plugging In on Grid-Ins

Plugging In is not just for multiple-choice questions. Take a look at the following question:

If m and n are both positive numbers and
$3m = 5n$, what is the value of $\dfrac{m - n}{m}$?

Pick numbers that make the math easy. If you make $m = 5$, then $3(5) = 5(n)$, so $n = 3$. Then find the value of the expression: $\dfrac{5 - 3}{5} = \dfrac{2}{5}$. That's all you have to do! The answer is $\dfrac{2}{5}$.

The numbers 5 and 3 were easy to use, but there are many numbers you could have used. For example, if you had used $m = 10$, then $30 = 5n$ would mean $n = 6$. Then the question would be what is $\dfrac{10 - 6}{10}$? Notice that this gives you $\dfrac{4}{10} = \dfrac{2}{5}$. The answer is the same no matter what you choose.

Try this one:

16

If $\dfrac{a}{b} = \dfrac{4}{7}$, and a and b are both positive numbers, what is the value of $\dfrac{b - a}{a + b}$?

The easiest numbers to plug in here are $a = 4$, and $b = 7$. Using these numbers gives you $\dfrac{7 - 4}{7 + 4} = \dfrac{3}{11}$. Since this is a grid-in, you're done!

HINT

When you see variables in the answers or in a grid-in question, it may be a good opportunity to PLUG IN!

Additional Ways to Plug In

Some questions will ask you to determine how a given function behaves. You can use Plugging In to help you make sense of the function and question.

Take a look at this question:

12

Krissi bakes cakes. The amount she charges, y, in dollars, for a cake with x servings is given by the equation $y = \dfrac{5x + 10}{2}$. How much does each additional serving cost a customer?

A) $2.50

B) $5.00

C) $10.00

D) $12.50

This question is trying to confuse you with the language, but try to plug in on it. Say she made a cake with 4 servings. You can plug in 4 for x to get $y = \dfrac{5(4) + 10}{2} = \dfrac{30}{2} = 15$. Now do the same with $x = 5$ for the additional serving to get $y = \dfrac{5(5) + 10}{2} = \dfrac{35}{2} = 17.5$. Therefore, the cost for one additional serving is $17.50 − $15 = $2.50, which is (A).

Calculators

Notice that the first and last questions above had

the image of a calculator beside them, but none

of the other questions did. This means that those

two questions were from a calculator-permitted

section, but the others were all from no-calculator

sections. Any questions in this book without a

calculator symbol are from no-calculator sections.

Of course, just because you can use your calculator

on this question doesn't mean that you should.

The calculations on the last question were pretty

straightforward and probably faster to do by hand

than typing into a calculator. Use your calculator

wisely. It's great for messier calculations like

$\frac{38.05}{7}$, but it will likely just slow you down on the

calculation $32 + (2 + 4)2 - (3-1)$.

Try another one:

16

$$A = \frac{1}{3}p + 60$$

The supply of apples for sale at a farmer's market is a function of the selling price of the apples. The equation above can be used to determine how many bushels of apples are for sale when the price of a bushel is p dollars. How will the quantity of apples for sale at the market change if the price of a bushel is increased by $30?

A) The number of bushels for sale will decrease by 10.

B) The number of bushels for sale will increase by 10.

C) The number of bushels for sale will increase by 30.

D) The number of bushels for sale will increase by 70.

Start by selecting a price for a bushel of apples. You want to choose a number that is divisible by 3 to make the math easy. Say a bushel costs $15. In this case the quantity of bushels for sale is $\frac{1}{3}(15) + 60 = 5 + 60 = 65$. If the price is increased by $30, the new price would be $45, and the number of bushels for sale would be $\frac{1}{3}(45) + 60 = 15 + 60 = 75$. The number of bushels for sale increased by 10. The answer is (B).

Similarly, if you are faced with a question that asks you to write an equation, you can use Plugging In to help you out.

Take a look at this question:

18

> Chelsea goes to the movies with her little brother. She has to purchase a ticket at full price, but her brother is a child and gets a 40% discount. She must then pay a tax of 7% on the whole purchase. Which of the following functions gives the total cost, C, that Chelsea will pay for two tickets if a full-price ticket costs p dollars?
>
> A) $C = 1.07p + 0.67p$
>
> B) $C = 1.07(2p - 0.4p)$
>
> C) $C = 1.07(2(0.6p))$
>
> D) $C = 1.07(2p - 0.4)$

You can make $p = 10$. Then Chelsea's brother's ticket would be $6. The total cost would be $16. Don't forget to add the tax: $16(1.07) = $17.12. Put $p = 10$ into the answers, and the only choice that works is (B).

Don't forget to check all four answers even if you find one that works! On tricky questions you may have to plug in more than once.

Here's another question to try:

21

A house painter estimates that it will take him x hours to paint a house. He promises the homeowner that the actual time will be within 8 hours of that estimate. If the painter keeps his promise and it takes him t hours to paint the whole house, which of the following inequalities accurately expresses the relationship between t and x ?

A) $|t - x| < 8$

B) $x + t < 8$

C) $x > t - 8$

D) $x < |t - 8|$

Say that the painter estimates that it will take 20 hours to complete the job, so $x = 20$. In this case t could be 27 hours and the estimate would be true. You can put these values into the answer choices and eliminate anything that is not true based on these numbers.

A) $|27 - 20| < 8$ Simplifies to $7 < 8$. This is true so keep it.

B) $20 + 27 < 8$ Simplifies to $47 < 8$. This is NOT true, so eliminate it.

C) $20 > 27 - 8$ Simplifies to $20 > 19$. This is true so keep it.

D) $20 < |27 - 8|$ Simplifies to $20 < 19$. This is NOT true, so eliminate it.

You still have two answers left, so try something different. Instead of using numbers that make his promise true, use numbers that make the problem *false*. The correct answer should NOT work with numbers that don't meet the painter's promise. Try plugging in $x = 20$ and $t = 10$ into the two remaining choices.

A) $|10 - 20| < 8$ Simplifies to $10 < 8$. Not true.

B) $x + t < 8$

C) $20 > 10 - 8$ This is still true, but it should not be. Eliminate it.

D) $x < |t - 8|$

The correct answer is (A).

Your Turn—Exercise 5.1

5

Anya makes 4 widgets per hour, and Carl makes 7 widgets per hour. If Anya works for a hours and Carl works for c hours, then which of the following represents the total number of widgets that Anya and Carl made?

A) $11ac$

B) $4c + 7a$

C) $28ac$

D) $4a + 7c$

8

If $\dfrac{c - 2d}{c} = \dfrac{5}{9}$, which of the following must also be true?

A) $\dfrac{c + d}{c} = \dfrac{13}{9}$

B) $\dfrac{d}{c} = \dfrac{2}{9}$

C) $\dfrac{d - 2c}{d} = -\dfrac{9}{5}$

D) $\dfrac{d - 2c}{d} = \dfrac{9}{5}$

9

If $\dfrac{x}{y} = 8$, what is the value of $\dfrac{12y}{x}$?

A) 1

B) $\dfrac{2}{3}$

C) $\dfrac{3}{2}$

D) 4

18

If $\dfrac{3x-2}{(x-4)^2} - \dfrac{3}{(x-4)} = \dfrac{a}{(x-4)^2}$ is true for

all values where $x \neq 4$, what is the value of a?

27

If a is the average (arithmetic mean) of x and 7, b is the average of $3x$ and 11, and c is the average of $2x$ and 6, what is the average of a, b, and c in terms of x?

A) $x + 4$

B) $x + 8$

C) $2x + 8$

D) $3x + 6$

Answers and Explanations to Exercise 5.1

5. **D** Plug in $a = 3$ and $c = 2$. Using these numbers Anya makes $(4)(3) = 12$ widgets, and Carl makes $7(2) = 14$ widgets. Together they make $12 + 14 = 26$ widgets. This is your target answer. Choice (A) gives you $11(3)(2) = 66$. Eliminate (A). Choice (B) gives you $4(2) + 7(3) = 29$; eliminate (B). Choice (C) gives you $28(6)$, which is way too big. Choice (D) gives you $4(3) + 7(2) = 12 + 14 = 26$. The answer is (D).

8. **B** Since the denominator is c on the left side and 9 on the right side, plug in 9 for c. This means that $9 - 2d = 5$, so $2d = 4$ and $d = 2$. Plug $c = 9$ and $d = 2$ into the answers and eliminate any that are not true. Eliminate (A) because $\dfrac{9 + 2}{9} \neq \dfrac{13}{9}$. Choice (B) is true, so keep it. Check (C): $\dfrac{2 - 2(9)}{2} = \dfrac{-16}{2} = -8 \neq \dfrac{-9}{5}$. Eliminate (C). You can eliminate (D) as well because it also gives you $\dfrac{2 - 2(9)}{2} = \dfrac{-16}{2} = -8$. The answer is (B).

9. **C** Plug in $x = 8$ and $y = 1$. This makes the expression $\dfrac{12}{8} = \dfrac{3}{2}$.

18. **10** Plug in $a = 2$: $\dfrac{3(2) - 2}{(2 - 4)^2} - \dfrac{3}{(2 - 4)} = \dfrac{a}{(2 - 4)^2}$.

This simplifies to $\dfrac{4}{4} - \left(\dfrac{3}{-2}\right) = \dfrac{a}{4}$, which is equal to

$\dfrac{4}{4} + \dfrac{3}{2} = \dfrac{4}{4} + \dfrac{6}{4} = \dfrac{10}{4}$. Therefore, $a = 10$.

27. **A** Plug in $x = 2$. If a is the average of 2 and 7, then

$a = \dfrac{2 + 7}{2} = \dfrac{9}{2} = 4.5$. If b is the average of $3x$ and 11,

then $b = \dfrac{6 + 11}{2} = \dfrac{17}{2} = 8.5$. Since c is the average of $2x$

and 6, $c = \dfrac{4 + 6}{2} = \dfrac{10}{2} = 5$. Lastly, the average of a, b, c

is $\dfrac{4.5 + 8.5 + 5}{3} = \dfrac{18}{3} = 6$. Only (A) matches this target

when $x = 2$, so it is the answer.

Plugging In the Answers

Consider the following question:

9

Mark goes to the store to buy a new computer. The computer is on sale for 40% off the original price. He then uses a coupon for an additional 15% off the sale price. If the total price (pre-tax) that he pays for the computer is $561, what was the original price of the computer?

A) $1100

B) $1020

C) $860

D) $730

You might be tempted to write your own equation, but because it's a multiple-choice question you don't need to! You can make use of the answers: Plug these values into the question and check the result. This eliminates the need to write an equation and helps reduce errors. Here's how Plugging In the Answers works:

Instead of starting with (A), start with (B). That way, if it's too high, you can eliminate (B), (C), and (D) and choose (A). If it's too low, you can eliminate (A) and (B).

Start with (B). If the original price of the computer was $1,020, then with a 40% discount it would be $1,020(0.6) = $612. Then with the 15% coupon, the final price would be $612(0.85) = $520.20. The computer was supposed to cost $561; therefore, this answer is not high enough, and the answer must be (A).

Try another:

7

> Cassidy and Jade write a paper together for a group project. If the paper is 37 pages long and Cassidy wrote 9 more pages than Jade did, how many pages did Cassidy write?
>
> A) 14
>
> B) 19
>
> C) 23
>
> D) 28

Start with (B) again and assume Cassidy wrote 19 pages. If Cassidy writes 19 pages and she writes 9 more pages than Jade, then Jade writes 10 pages. Together they would write 29 pages. This number is not high enough since the paper is 37 pages. Eliminate (A) and (B). Try (C). If Cassidy writes 23 pages, then Jade must have written 14 pages. Together they would write 23 + 14 = 37 pages. This works, so the answer is (C). When plugging in the answers, there is no need to keep going after you find an answer that works.

Sometimes even when an equation (or inequality) is given, plugging in the answers is easier and faster than solving it.

Take a look at the following question:

6

Which of the following values is a solution of
$\frac{1}{5}(7x - 3) < x$?

A) 4

B) 3

C) 2

D) 1

Since this is an inequality, you don't need to start with (B), but rather with either the largest or smallest value. Since the left side will increase more rapidly than the right side, and you want the left side to be less than the value of x, it makes more sense to start with (D), the smallest number, than (A). Plug in $x = 1$ to get $\frac{1}{5}(7 - 3) < 1$, which is $\frac{4}{5} < 1$. This statement is true, so the answer is (D). Even if you didn't see to start with (D), the calculations are easy, so it wouldn't take long to work through the answers.

Your Turn—Exercise 5.2

25

Mark decreases the width of his rectangular farm plot by 20% and increases the length of it by x%. If these changes increase the area of the farm plot by 8%, then what is the value of x ?

A) 16

B) 24

C) 35

D) 40

23

Kaitlyn takes a test with both a multiple-choice section and a short answer section. She receives 20% more points on the short answer section than the multiple-choice section, and she scores a total of 88 points on the test. How many points did she receive on the multiple-choice section?

A) 34

B) 40

C) 48

D) 68

28

An art teacher has x students in her art class. She has a total budget of y dollars to spend on art supplies for the class. If she spends \$4 on supplies per student, then she will be \$3 under budget. However, if she spends \$5 per student, then she will be \$18 over budget. How many students are in the art class?

A) 15

B) 18

C) 21

D) 30

7

$$|x - 3| + 2 = 0$$

For what value of x is the above equation true?

A) −2

B) 1

C) 3

D) There is no value of x for which the statement is true.

Answers and Explanations to Exercise 5.2

25. **C** For this question you can use a combination of Plugging In and Plugging In the Answers. Start by drawing a farm plot for Mark that is 10 ft by 10 ft. This way it has an area of 100. If he decreases the width by 20%, then the new width would be $10(0.8) = 8$ feet. Now, Plug In the Answers to find the new length. Start with (B). If the length is increased by 24%, then the new length is $10(1.24) = 12.4$ feet. The new area would be $8(12.4) = 99.2$ feet. This actually decreased the size of his farm plot, so he must increase the length by more than this. Eliminate (A) and (B). Try (C). The new length would be $10(1.35) = 13.5$, and then new area would be $8(13.5) = 108$ feet. This is 8% greater than the original area of 100 square feet, so the answer is (C).

23. **B** Start with (B). If she scores 40 points on the multiple-choice section, then she scores 20% more than this, or $40(1.20) = 48$ points, on the short answer section. Therefore, she scores a total of 88 points. This matches the information in the question, so the answer is (B).

28. **C** Start with (B). If she has 18 students in her class and spends $4 per student, then she will spend 18(4) = 72 dollars. This is $3 less than her budget, so the budget is $75. If she spends $5 on each of these 18 students, then she will spend $90, which is $15 over budget. She was supposed to be $18 over budget, so there must be more than 18 students in the class. Eliminate (A) and (B), and try (C). She spends $4 on each of her 21 students for a total of $84 dollars, so her budget is $87. If she spends $5 on each of the 21 students, then she will spend $105, which is $18 over budget. The answer is (C).

7. **D** Try each of the values given. Choice (A) gives you $|-5| + 2 = 0$, which becomes $5 + 2 = 0$. This is not true. Choice (B) $|-2| + 2 = 0$, which simplifies to $2 + 2 = 0$. This not true. Choice (C) is $|0| + 2 = 0$. This is also not true. The answer is (D).

Step 6: Mastering the Fundamentals

A lot of the math on the SAT will require you to interpret and manipulate equations and inequalities. You'll also have to work with fractions, exponents, roots, quadratics, and polynomials. This chapter provides a refresher on all of the basics that you need to know. It will also help you strengthen your skills in these areas and practice applying them to SAT style questions.

Equations and Inequalities

Interpreting Values in Equations

On the SAT, you'll be expected to interpret the meanings of coefficients and constants in equations that model real-world scenarios.

A **coefficient** is the number in front of a variable. The coefficient represents a rate of change, i.e. the amount that the value increases or decreases for one additional unit of the variable.

A **constant** term does not include a variable and, therefore, does not vary.

Consider the following:

> Kelly opens a bank account with an initial deposit and then makes a fixed deposit into the account once per week. The equation $B = 30x + 150$ models the amount of money in Kelly's bank account x weeks after she opens it.

The *coefficient* is 30, and the *constant* term is 150.

In this case, the coefficient means that each month Kelly adds an additional $30 to her bank account. The 150 represents the initial deposit, which is the value when x is 0.

Similarly, the equation $B = 150 - 30x$ would be used to model the scenario in which she removes $30 from the account each week.

Take a look at this question:

9

Mike is reading a book. The number of pages that he has left to read, P, is given by the equation $P = 530 - 57t$, where t represents the number of days since he started reading the book. What are the meanings of 530 and 57 in this equation?

A) It will take Mike 530 days to read the book at a rate of 57 pages per day.

B) The book has 530 pages, and Mike reads 57 pages a day.

C) Mike reads the book, which has 530 pages, at a rate of 57 pages per hour.

D) After 57 days, Mike has read 530 pages of the book.

Take it one step at a time:

The coefficient 57 represents a rate, not a number of days, so eliminate (D).

Watch your units; it says that t is the number of *days*, so you can eliminate (C).

Lastly, when $t = 0$, Mike has 530 pages left to read. Therefore, the book must have 530 pages. The answer is (B).

Creating Equations and Inequalities

Sometimes the test writers won't give you the equation at all, but instead will ask you to create one. To do this you need to translate English to Math. Use the same principles: a rate should be a coefficient, but initial values such as the number of members in a club or the opening balance of a checking account should be constants that are not attached to a variable. The following chart shows a few additional helpful tips to keep in mind:

English	Math Equivalent
% (Percent)	$\dfrac{x}{100}$
Of	$\times$
Is/are/were/did/does	$=$
Out of	$\div$
Per	$\times$
More than/greater than	$>$
Less than/fewer than	$<$
At least/no less than	$\leq$
At most/up to/no more than	$\geq$

Take a look at this question:

11

> A bathtub that can hold up to 80 gallons currently has 13 gallons of water in it. Water flows into the bathtub at a rate of 7.5 gallons per minute. If t represents the time, in minutes, since the faucet was turned on, which of the following inequalities represents all of the time before the bathtub begins to overflow?
>
> A) $80 - 13t > 7.5$
>
> B) $7.5 + 13t \leq 80$
>
> C) $80 - 7.5t < 13$
>
> D) $7.5t + 13 \leq 80$

Since this is a multiple-choice question, you should start with the easiest piece of information and use POE. The water flows at a rate of 7.5 gallons per minute. Since this is a rate per minute, it should be a coefficient to the variable t. Eliminate (A) and (B) because the coefficient is 13 instead of 7.5. If the tub currently holds 13 gallons and water flows into the tub at a rate of $7.5t$, then the tub has a volume of $13 + 7.5t$. The question asks for the time *before* it over-flows, so you need this value to be less than or equal to the maximum capacity of 80 gallons. This matches (D).

Alternatively, once you had narrowed down your choices to (C) and (D), you could have plugged in $t = 0$. The tub is not yet overflowing, so the inequality should be true using $t = 0$, but (C) is false.

Try one more:

20

A company that makes flavored juice drinks has two flavors of juice. Juice M is 71% water, and juice N is 63% water. The company wants to make a blend with at most 9 cups of juice that is no more than 66% water. If m represents the number of cups of juice M, and n represents the number of cups of juice N, which of the following systems represents all of the possible blends the company can make that fit these constraints?

A) $m > 0$
$n > 0$
$m + n = 9$
$$\frac{71m + 63n}{m + n} \geq 66$$

B) $0 \leq m \leq 9$
$0 \leq n \leq 9$
$71m + 63n \leq 66(m + n)$

C) $m > 0$
$n > 0$
$m + n \leq 9$
$71m + 63n \leq 66(m + n)$

D) $m > 0$
$n > 0$
$m + n \leq 9$
$71m + 63n \geq 66(m + n)$

Start with the most straightforward piece of information. The company wants to make at most 9 cups of juice, so m cups + n cups is less than or equal to 9: $m + n \leq 9$. Eliminate (A) and (B) because they do not contain this inequality. Between (C) and (D), the only difference is the $\leq$ or $\geq$. The question says "no more than 66%" which means less than or equal to, so the correct answer is (C). Using POE and starting with the straightforward pieces first, you were able to avoid dealing with the more complicated aspects of writing these inequalities.

While POE is a great strategy for multiple-choice questions, sometimes you'll be given grid-ins that require you to write and solve an equation. Try to write an equation that represents each of the following statements.

1. If 18 is added to three times a number a, the result is 12.

   _____

2. $2x + 9$ is 6 less than 21.

   _____

3. There are 190 juniors and 420 seniors with parking permits at a school. If x more juniors receive parking permits, then $\frac{2}{5}$ of the students with parking permits will be juniors.

   _____

Answers:

1. $18 + 3a = 12$

2. $2x + 9 = 21 - 6$

3. $190 + x = \dfrac{2}{5}(190 + x + 420)$, which simplifies to $190 + x = \dfrac{2}{5}(610 + x)$

This last one is pretty tricky, but take it one step at a time. There are currently 190 juniors with parking permits, so if x more receive permits, then the total number of juniors with permits is $190 + x$. This value needs to be equal to $\dfrac{2}{5}$ of the total students with parking permits, which translates to $\dfrac{2}{5} \times$ (juniors with permits + seniors with permits). When you put all of this together you get $190 + x = \dfrac{2}{5}(190 + x + 420)$, or $190 + x = \dfrac{2}{5}(610 + x)$. Alternatively, you may have written it as a proportion: $\dfrac{\textit{juniors with permits}}{\textit{juniors and seniors with permits}} = \dfrac{2}{5}$ which would be $\dfrac{190 + x}{610 + x} = \dfrac{2}{5}$.

Manipulating Equations

Now that you've mastered writing equations, what might you need to do with them?

Take a look at this question:

13

An instructor calculates a student's score, S, on a test using the formula $\dfrac{R}{R + W} = S$, in which R is the number of questions a student got right and W is the number of questions a student got wrong. Which of the following equations gives the number of questions a student got right in terms of the other variables?

A) $R = \dfrac{SW}{1 - S}$

B) $R = \dfrac{SW}{S - 1}$

C) $R = \dfrac{W}{1 - S}$

D) $R = \dfrac{S}{W - 1}$

This question asks you to isolate the variable R. As you do this, the main rule to keep in mind is that whatever you do to one side of the equation, you must do to the other side as well.

Start by getting rid of the fraction. In order to get rid of the fraction on the left side you need to multiply it by the denominator $(R + W)$. You must also do the same to the right side of the equation:

$$\frac{R}{R + W}(R + W) = S(R + W)$$

This simplifies to $R = SR + SW$.

Next, gather both of the R terms onto the left side by subtracting SR from both sides:

$$R - SR = SW$$

Now, since both terms on the left have an R in them, you can rewrite the left side:

$$R(1 - S) = SW$$

The final step is to divide both sides by $(1 - S)$:

$$\frac{R(1 - S)}{(1 - S)} = \frac{SW}{(1 - S)}, \text{ which simplifies to } R = \frac{SW}{(1 - S)}$$

The correct answer is (A).

Try one more:

3

$$p = 89.49 + 5.60n$$

The cost for cable TV service for a home depends on the number of TVs that are connected to the cable service. The equation above shows the relationship between the total price of the service, p, and the number of TVs, n. Which of the following expresses the number of TVs in terms of the total price of the service?

A) $n = \dfrac{p + 89.49}{5.60}$

B) $n = \dfrac{p - 89.49}{5.60}$

C) $n = \dfrac{89.49 - p}{5.60}$

D) $n = \dfrac{5.60}{p - 89.49}$

You want to isolate the n, so subtract 89.49 from both sides:

$$p - 89.49 = 5.60n$$

Now, divide both sides by 5.60:

$$\dfrac{p - 89.49}{5.60} = n,$$ which is the same thing as (B).

You could have chosen to subtract the $5.60n$ from both sides first, but this would have required more steps:

$$p - 5.60n = 89.49 \; ; \; -5.60n = 89.49 - p \; ;$$

$$n = \frac{89.49 - p}{-5.60} \; ; \; n = \frac{-89.49 + p}{5.60} \; ; \; n = \frac{p - 89.49}{5.60}$$

It doesn't matter which side of the equation you isolate the variable on, so do whichever is easier for you.

Solving Equations and Inequalities

When the SAT actually asks you to solve equations, you follow the same idea: isolate the variable of interest, and whatever you do to one side, do the same to the other.

HINT

Before you start rearranging terms, make sure to check what the question is actually asking.

You may see a question like this:

$7(a + b) = 3$, what is the value of $a + b$?

In this case, you don't care about isolating the a or the b, you just need to divide both sides by 7!

Here are a few additional things to keep in mind.

Distributing

The Distributive Property states that $x(a + b) = xa + xb$.

For example, $3(x + 2) = 3x + 6$.

Most of the mistakes people make when using the distributive property involve negative signs. Don't forget to distribute the negative sign!

For example, $-3(x - 2) = (-3)x - (-3)2 = -3x - (-6) = -3x + 6$.

Use the distributive property to simplify each of the following:

1. $7(x - 2) + 4(x + 2) =$ _____

2. $3(2x + 4) - 3(2 - x) =$ _____

3. $-3x(2x - 3) =$ _____

Answers:

1. $[7(x) - 7(2)] + [4(x) + 4(2)] = (7x - 14) + (4x + 8) = 11x - 6$

2. $[3(2x) + 3(4)] - [3(2) - 3(x)] = (6x + 12) - (6 - 3x) = 9x + 6$

3. $(-3x)(2x) - (-3x)(3) = -6x^2 - (-9x) = -6x^2 + 9x$

Clearing Fractions

Sometimes you can make your work a lot easier by clearing the fractions before you do any other work. For example, the first step in solving $\frac{1}{3}(4x-5) = x$ is to multiply both sides by 3 to get rid of the fraction. This gives you $4x - 5 = 3x$.

This same principle applies even when you have multiple denominators in an equation.

Take a look at this question:

16

If $\frac{5}{4}x + 2 = \frac{7}{3}x$, what is the value of x ?

Instead of trying to add and subtract fractions, you can multiply the whole equation by a common denominator. A *common denominator* is a number that is a multiple of both denominators. In this case 12 would work. If you multiply the entire equation by 12, it looks like this:

$\frac{(12)5}{4}x + (12)2 = \frac{(12)7}{3}x$ = which simplifies to $3(5)x + 24 = 4(7)x$

or $15x + 24 = 28x$.

Now you can solve the equation without having to add or subtract fractions!

Subtract $15x$ from both sides:

$$24 = 13x$$

Divide by 13:

$$x = \frac{24}{13}$$

Try to clear the fractions from these two equations yourself:

1. $2x + \dfrac{1}{3} = 3 + \dfrac{1}{6}x$ _____

2. $\dfrac{3(x-1)}{4} + \dfrac{5}{2} = 9$ _____

Answers:

1. Multiply by 6: $12x + 2 = 18 + x$

2. Multiply by 4: $3(x-1) + 10 = 36$

Flipping the Sign in Inequalities

Using algebra to solve inequalities is the same as using algebra to solve equations, with one important extra rule. If you divide or multiply by a negative while solving an inequality, you have to flip the inequality sign.

Take a look at the following question. It would be a multiple-choice question, but let's ignore the answers to focus on solving the inequality.

17

If $5x - 7 \leq 7x + 3$, what is one possible value of x?

To solve this, add 7 to both sides:

$$5x \leq 7x + 10$$

And then subtract $7x$ from each side:

$$-2x \leq 10$$

The last step is to isolate x by dividing both sides by -2. Since you are dividing by a negative value, you must flip the sign:

$$x \geq -5.$$

Try solving these two yourself:

1. $2x - 3 \geq 3x - 2$ _____

2. $\frac{1}{3}x + 2 < 2x + 7$ _____

Answers:

1. Subtract $3x$ from both sides: $-x - 3 \geq -2$. Add 3 to both sides: $-x \geq 1$. Divide by -1 and flip the sign: $x \leq -1$

2. Clear the fraction by multiplying by 3: $x + 6 < 6x + 21$. Subtract $6x$: $-5x + 6 < 21$. Subtract 6: $-5x < 15$. Divide by -5 and flip the sign: $x > -3$.

Systems of Equations

Sometimes you'll be given two equations and two variables to solve. This may seem like twice as much work, but luckily it usually isn't. Just **Stack and Add**!

Take a look at the following problem:

$$2x - y = 9$$
$$3x + y = 6$$

If (x, y) is a solution to the system of equations above, what is the value of x?

Since the question asks for the value of x, you want to eliminate y from the equation. You can do this by adding the two equations:

$$\begin{array}{r} 2x - y = 9 \\ + \quad 3x + y = 6 \\ \hline 5x \quad = 15 \end{array}$$

The y terms cancel out, and the final step is just to divide by 5: $x = 3$.

Try another:

$$-2x + 4y = 8$$
$$4x - 3y = 12$$

If (x, y) is a solution to the system of
equations above, what is the value of x?

Check which variable the question is asking about first. Since the question asks you for the x value, you should try to eliminate the y terms. In this case, you need to multiply each equation by a constant term in order to get the y values to cancel out. Multiply the top equation by 3 and the bottom equation by 4:

$3[-2x + 4y = 8]$ gives you $-6x + 12y = 24$

$4[4x - 3y = 4]$ gives you $16x - 12y = 16$

Now you can Stack and Add:

$$-6x + 12y = 24$$
$$\underline{+\ \ 16x - 12y = 16}$$
$$10x\qquad\ \ = 40$$

Lastly, divide by 10 to get $x = 4$.

Try to use Stack and Add to solve for each of the following:

1. $2x + y = -5$
   $x + y = -10$

   What is the value of y? _____

2. $4x + 5y = 15$
   $3x + 2y = 6$

   What is the value of $x + y$? _____

Answers:

1. Multiply the second equation by (-2) to get $-2x - 2y = 20$. Now add the equations to get $-y = 15$; $y = -15$.

2. Add both equations to get $7x + 7y = 21$. Divide by 7 to get $x + y = 3$. Make sure to always check what the question is asking—do not isolate a variable if you don't need to!

Your Turn—Exercise 6.1

11

$$P = 1,216 - 323n$$

The equation above estimates the total profit, P, in millions, of a cell phone provider in the nth year after it hires its new CEO. What does the 323 in the equation represent?

A) Every year the number of customers decreases by 323.

B) For every decrease of 323 customers, the company loses $1,216 in profit.

C) Every year the profit of the company decreases by $323,000.

D) Every year the profit of the company decreases by $323,000,000.

13

$$D = \frac{9}{8} E - 2.75$$

Ron is traveling to Italy from the United States. When he goes to an ATM to withdraw euros, the bank uses the above formula to calculate the number of dollars, D, that his account will be charged if he withdraws E euros. Based on the equation, which of the following must be true?

I. For each additional $\frac{9}{8}$ of a euro that he withdraws, he will be charged one additional dollar.

II. For each additional dollar Ron is charged, he receives $\frac{8}{9}$ of a euro from the ATM.

III. For each additional euro that Ron withdraws, he will be charged an additional $\frac{9}{8}$ of a dollar.

A) I only

B) III only

C) I and II only

D) II and III only

33

A plane can carry no more than 500 pounds. If the plane has 2 passengers with a combined weight of 275 pounds, what is the maximum number of bags that they can put on the plane if each bag weighs 29 pounds?

34

A pool has 800 gallons of water in it currently. If the pool is leaking at a rate of 12 gallons per hour, then how many gallons will be in the pool after 48 hours?

10

What is the value of p if $\dfrac{5(p-1)}{4} - 1 = 0$?

A) $\dfrac{5}{9}$

B) 1

C) $\dfrac{5}{4}$

D) $\dfrac{9}{5}$

12

$$5x - 2 \leq 7x + 4$$

Which of the following is NOT a solution to the inequality above?

A) −1

B) −2

C) −3

D) −4

8

$$5x + 6y = -19$$
$$3y + 2x = -13$$

What is the solution (x, y) to the system of equations above?

A) $(13, -14)$

B) $(-5, -1)$

C) $(7, -9)$

D) $(5, -9)$

17

A bagel shop sells only bagels and coffee. The bagels sell for $1.50 each and coffee for $3.00 a cup. If the bagel shop's revenue for a total of 521 items one morning was $1,228.50, how many bagels were sold that morning?

A) 223

B) 276

C) 298

D) 312

4

$$\frac{y}{x} = 5$$
$$y = 3(x - 2)$$

What is the value of x in the solution to the system of equations above?

A) −3

B) −2

C) 1

D) 3

Answers and Explanations to Exercise 6.1

11. **D** The equation refers to profit, not number of customers, so eliminate (A) and (B). The question states that the equation P is in *millions*, so each year the company's profit is decreasing by $323,000,000.

13. **D** The coefficient on E is $\frac{9}{8}$, so this means that for each additional E, the value of D increases by $\frac{9}{8}$. This is what statement III says, so eliminate (A) and (C) because you know III must be true. Look at your remaining answer choices; you actually do not need to check statement I (which is not true because it is the reverse of III). Statement II means the same thing as statement III. If you weren't sure, you could check it by rearranging the terms to isolate E: First, clear the fraction by multiplying both sides by 8: $8D = 9E - 8(2.75)$; $8D + 8(2.75) = 9E$; $\frac{8}{9}D + \frac{8(2.75)}{9} = E$. The coefficient on D is $\frac{8}{9}$, which means that for each increase of D, the value of E increases by $\frac{8}{9}$. Both II and III are correct; the answer is (D). Note that you could have ignored the constant term altogether since you cared only about the coefficient for this problem.

33. **7** This translates to $275 + 29x \leq 500$. Subtract 275 from both sides: $29x \leq 225$. Divide by 29: $x \leq 7.76$. You cannot round up to 8 because the value cannot be higher than 7.76. Therefore, the answer is 7.

34. **224**

To solve this problem you need to translate this word problem into your own equation. The pool started with 800 gallons but is leaking at a rate of 12 gallons per hour. The coefficient should be –12, and the constant should be 800. Your equation for volume, in which t represents the number of hours, should look like this: $V = 800 - 12t$. Therefore, after 48 hours, the volume would be $800 - 12(48) = 224$.

10. **D** Start by adding 1 to both sides to get $\dfrac{5(p-1)}{4} = 1$. Now you can get rid of the denominator by multiplying both sides by 4 to get $5(p - 1) = 4$. Now you can distribute to get $5p - 5 = 4$. Add 5 to both sides: $5p = 9$. Finally, divide by 5 to get $p = \dfrac{9}{5}$.

12. **D** Start by adding 2 to both sides to get $5x \leq 7x + 6$. Now, subtract $7x$ from both sides: $-2x \leq 6$. Finally, divide by –2, but don't forget to flip the sign since you are dividing by a negative. The solution is $x \geq -3$. The question asks for the value that is NOT a solution, so the answer is (D).

8. **C** Before you can stack and add these equations, you need to get them in the same form. Rewrite the second equation so that the x term is listed first: $2x + 3y = -13$. Now that the equations are in the same form, check the answer choices. Since the x values are all different, the best strategy is to solve for x by eliminating y in the bottom equation. In order to do this you need the coefficient on y to be -6, so you should multiply the bottom equation by -2:

$-2[-2x + 3y = -13]$ gives you $-4x - 6y = 26$

Now stack these two equations on top of each other and add:

$$\begin{array}{rl} 5x + 6y = & -19 \\ + \ -4x - 6y = & 26 \\ \hline x \quad\quad = & 7 \end{array}$$

Only (C) has $x = 7$.

17. **A** You can translate this word problem into a system of equations. If b is the number of bagels and c is the number of cups of coffee sold, then the revenue would be given by $1.5b + 3c = 1,228.5$. The number of items sold was 521, so $b + c = 521$. You want to know the value of b, so you want the coefficient on c in the second equation to be -3. To do this, multiply the second equation by -3: $-3[b + c = 521]$ gives you $-3b - 3c = -1,563$. Now you can Stack and Add:

$$\begin{array}{rl} 1.5b + \ 3c = & 1,228.50 \\ + \ -3b - \ 3c = & -1,563 \\ \hline -1.5b \quad\quad = & -334.5 \end{array}$$

Divide by -1.5 to get $b = 223$. The answer is (A).

Alternatively, you could probably solve this problem faster by plugging in the answer. Start with (B). If the shop sold 276 bagels for $1.50 each, they would make $414 on bagels. If they sell a total of 521 items, then they would sell 521 − 276 = 245 cups of coffee. At $3 each, this would net $735. Add the two revenues together to get $735 + $414 = $1,149. Since this is not enough profit, the shop must have sold fewer of the cheaper product, bagels, and more of the coffee. Therefore, the answer is (A).

4. **A** Even though this system of equations does not work well with Stack and Add, you can still solve it with minimal work. Rewrite the first equation to isolate the y: $y = 5x$. Now all you have to do is set the two equations equal to one another and solve for x: $5x = 3(x − 2)$. Distribute the 3 to get $5x = 3x − 6$. Subtract $3x$ from each side to get $2x = − 6$. Finally, divide by 2 to get $x = −3$. The answer is (A).

Fractions and Rational Expressions

You'll likely see a lot of fractions on the SAT, so here's a quick refresher on working with fractions.

Adding and Subtracting Fractions

In order to add or subtract fractions, you need a common denominator. The *denominator* is the value on the bottom of the fraction.

For example, to solve $\frac{3}{4} + \frac{7}{8}$, you need to make the denominator of the first fraction 8 as well. In order to do this, you need to multiply the denominator by 2. Since you don't want to change the value of the fraction, you must multiply the *numerator* (the value on the top of the fraction) by 2 as well: $\frac{3}{4} = \frac{(2)3}{(2)4} = \frac{6}{8}$. Now you can add the two fractions: $\frac{6}{8} + \frac{7}{8} = \frac{13}{8}$. Notice that you add only the numerators; the denominator remains the same.

In this example it was easy to find the common denominator since 8 is a multiple of 4. Oftentimes that is not the case though. For example, consider $\frac{3}{11} + \frac{2}{5}$. The easiest way to solve this problem is with the bowtie method. It's called the bowtie method because of the way it looks when you finish.

(1.)

$$\frac{3}{11} + \frac{2}{5} = \frac{15}{}$$

(2.)

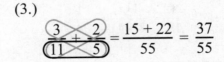

$$\frac{3}{11} + \frac{2}{5} = \frac{15 + 22}{}$$

(3.)

$$\frac{3}{11} + \frac{2}{5} = \frac{15 + 22}{55} = \frac{37}{55}$$

(1) Multiply the left numerator with the right denominator. Write this number in the numerator on the other side of the equal sign as shown.

(2) Next, multiply the right numerator with the left denominator. This product also goes in the numerator of the right side of the equal sign. If you are adding the two fractions, put a plus sign between these numbers. If you are subtracting them, then put a minus sign.

(3) Lastly, multiply the two denominators and put this number in the denominator on the right side of the equal sign. Now just add or subtract the two numbers in your numerator and you're done.

Reducing Fractions

In the example above, $\frac{37}{55}$ is in its simplest form, but sometimes you'll need to reduce a fraction by dividing both the numerator and denominator by a common factor.

Try this one:

$$\frac{5}{6} - \frac{3}{8} =$$

Using the bowtie method you get: $\frac{5(8) - 6(3)}{6(8)} = \frac{40 - 18}{48} = \frac{22}{48}$.

Since both 22 and 40 share a common factor of 2, you can reduce

this fraction as shown: $\frac{22}{48} = \frac{2(11)}{2(24)} = \frac{11}{24}$.

HINT

On multiple-choice questions the answers will likely be in reduced form. On a grid-in you do not need to reduce a fraction unless there is not room to grid it in. For example, you would not have room to grid in the fraction $\frac{18}{10}$, so you would need to reduce it to $\frac{9}{5}$. However, if your answer is $\frac{9}{27}$, you could grid it in without needing to reduce it to $\frac{1}{3}$.

Multiplying and Dividing Fractions

Multiplying fractions is actually much simpler than adding or subtracting. All you have to do is multiply the numerators across and multiply the denominators across.

$$\frac{3}{8} \times \frac{2}{5} = \frac{(3)(2)}{(8)(5)} = \frac{6}{40} = \frac{3}{20}$$

Following this idea, to square a fraction you square both the numerator and the denominator:

$$\left(\frac{3}{8}\right)^2 = \frac{3}{8} \times \frac{3}{8} = \frac{9}{64}$$

Dividing fractions is not much harder. To divide by a fraction, just multiply the first fraction by the *reciprocal* of the second fraction. The reciprocal of a fraction is the value that results when you switch the numerator and the denominator. The reciprocal of $\frac{3}{4}$ is $\frac{4}{3}$.

$$\frac{5}{9} \div \frac{4}{7} = \frac{5}{9} \times \frac{7}{4} = \frac{35}{36}$$

Your Turn—Exercise 6.2

Try to solve each of the problems below and reduce the fractions if possible.

1. $\dfrac{2}{3} \times \dfrac{3}{4} - \dfrac{5}{6} =$ _____

2. $\left(\dfrac{2}{3}\right)^2 + \dfrac{7}{8} =$ _____

3. $\dfrac{12}{\frac{3}{5}} =$ _____

Answers and Explanations to Exercise 6.2

1. Do the multiplication first: $\frac{2}{3} \times \frac{3}{4} = \frac{6}{12}$. Now, convert the $\frac{5}{6}$ to $\frac{10}{12}$ so you have a common denominator of 12. The equation becomes $\frac{6}{12} - \frac{10}{12} = \frac{-4}{12} = \frac{-1}{3}$.

2. Square the first term: $\left(\frac{2}{3}\right)^2 = \frac{2}{3} \times \frac{2}{3} = \frac{4}{9}$. Then use the bowtie method to add: $\frac{4}{9} + \frac{7}{8} = \frac{4(8) + 7(9)}{9(8)} = \frac{32 + 63}{72} = \frac{95}{72}$.

3. Rewrite this equation as $\frac{12}{1} \div \frac{3}{5} = \frac{12}{1} \times \frac{5}{3} = \frac{60}{3} = 20$.

Now that you're an expert at working with fractions, take a look at this question:

18

$$\frac{3}{7}x + \frac{1}{4} = \frac{7}{12} + \frac{1}{7}x$$

What is the value of x in the equation above?

This question can look intimidating with all the different denominators, but if you apply all the rules you just reviewed, you can get through it without too much hassle. First, gather your x terms on the left side by subtracting $\frac{1}{7}x$ from both sides to get $\frac{3}{7}x - \frac{1}{7}x + \frac{1}{4} = \frac{7}{12}$.

Then, subtract $\frac{1}{4}$ from each side to get $\frac{3}{7}x - \frac{1}{7}x = \frac{7}{12} - \frac{1}{4}$.

Since the left side already has a common denominator, just subtract the numerators to get $\frac{2}{7}x = \frac{7}{12} - \frac{1}{4}$. You can now use 12 as a common denominator on the right side: $\frac{2}{7}x = \frac{7}{12} - \frac{(3)1}{(3)4} = \frac{7}{12} - \frac{3}{12}$.

The equation is now $\frac{2}{7}x = \frac{4}{12}$, which simplifies to $\frac{2}{7}x = \frac{1}{3}$.

Lastly, divide both sides by $\frac{2}{7}$ by multiplying by the reciprocal:

$x = \frac{1}{3} \div \frac{2}{7} = \frac{1}{3} \times \frac{7}{2} = \frac{7}{6}$. Therefore, the answer is $x = \frac{7}{6}$.

Rational Expressions

A *rational expression* is just a fraction in which the numerator and/or denominator is a polynomial instead of a single term (a *polynomial* is an expression with two or more terms). Rational expressions follow all the same rules as other fractions.

Consider the following:

$$\frac{2x}{x + 2} + \frac{x}{3}$$

In order to add these two expressions you should use the bowtie method:

$$\frac{2x}{x + 2} + \frac{x}{3} = \frac{2x(3) + x(x + 2)}{3(x + 2)} = \frac{6x + x^2 + 2x}{3x + 6} = \frac{8x + x^2}{3x + 6}$$

You simplify a rational expression the same way that you reduce a fraction: divide out any common factors.

$$\frac{3x^2 + 9x}{6x} = \frac{3x(x + 3)}{3x(2)} = \frac{x + 3}{2}$$

Splitting Rational Expressions

When you have a polynomial in the numerator, you can split a rational expression into the sum of multiple fractions. Consider the example above. You could alternatively have written $\frac{x + 3}{2}$ as $\frac{x}{2} + \frac{3}{2}$.

Take a look at another:

$$\frac{2x - 3}{4x^2 + 2x} = \frac{2x}{4x^2 + 2x} - \frac{3}{4x^2 + 2x}$$

You could now factor out $2x$ from the first expression to get $\frac{1}{2x + 1} - \frac{3}{4x^2 + 2x}$. All three of these are equivalent ways to write the same rational expression.

HINT

You can split the numerator, but you can never split the denominator!

$$\frac{2x}{x + 3} \neq \frac{2x}{x} + \frac{2x}{3}$$

Cross-Multiplying

When you have a rational expression or fraction on both sides of an equal sign, you can cross-multiply and set the products equal to each other.

Take a look at the following question:

7

If $\dfrac{4x - 1}{3x} = \dfrac{2}{3}$, what is the value of $4x$?

A) $\dfrac{1}{2}$

B) 1

C) 2

D) 3

Cross-multiply to get $(4x - 1)3 = 2(3x)$, which simplifies to $12x - 3 = 6x$.

You can now solve for x by adding 3 to both sides to get $12x = 6x + 3$, then subtracting $6x$ to get $6x = 3$, and dividing by 6 to get $x = \dfrac{1}{2}$. Finally, don't forget that the question asked for $4x$, not x, so the answer is $4x = 2$, (C).

Try one yourself:

16

If $\dfrac{2x}{3} = \dfrac{x + 5}{4}$, what is the value of x?

Answer: Cross-multiply to get $8x = 3x + 15$. Subtract $3x$ from both sides to get $5x = 15$. Divide by 5 to get $x = 3$.

Unit Conversions and Proportions

Cross-multiplying is especially useful with proportions. When the ratio between two variables is constant, you can solve them with a proportion. For example, the amount of money that a lifeguard makes and the number of hours that he works are directly proportional. If a lifeguard makes $35 for 4 hours of work, then he would make $70 for 8 hours of work. Notice how this relationship can be represented with a proportion.

$$\frac{\$35}{4 \ hours} = \frac{\$70}{8 \ hours}$$

You can apply this concept to questions in which the relationship is not as obvious as it was in this example. Consider the following question:

> A lifeguard makes $35 for 4 hours of work. Approximately how many hours does he need to work to make $250? (Round to the nearest hundredth.)

It sounds a lot more complicated than the first example, but the only difference is that you can't visualize it as well. It's actually exactly the same idea. All you have to do is set up a proportion and then use cross-multiplication.

$$\frac{\$35}{4} = \frac{\$250}{x} \qquad 35x = (4)250; \ 35x = 1,000; \ x \approx 28.57$$

Try the following question:

3

An employee at a clothing store is paid a commission based on the amount of merchandise she sells. She makes $13 on a sale of $300 of merchandise. At this rate, how much commission does she make in a week if she sells $12,000 of merchandise?

A) $400

B) $460

C) $520

D) $560

Since the question says the rate is the same, you can set up a proportion. Put the commission in the numerator and the merchandise in the denominator: $\dfrac{\$13}{\$300} = \dfrac{x}{\$12,000}$. Cross-multiply to get $13(12,000) = 300x$; $156,000 = 300x$. Finally, divide by 300 to get $x = \$520$.

You can also use proportions to solve unit conversion problems.

Take a look at the following question:

4

> A car can travel up to 28.5 kilometers on one
> gallon of gas. Approximately how far can it
> travel on one gallon of gas in <u>miles</u>?
> (1 mile ≈ 1.61 kilometers)
>
> A) 15.45
>
> B) 17.70
>
> C) 26.89
>
> D) 45.88

Set up a proportion with miles in the numerators and kilometers in

the denominators: $\dfrac{1\ mile}{1.61\ kilometers} = \dfrac{x\ miles}{28.5\ kilometers}$

Now you can cross-multiply to get $28.5 = 1.61x$. Divide by 1.61 to
get $x = 17.70$.

It can be helpful on unit conversions to use logic to eliminate some
answers before you calculate as well. Since miles are longer than kilometers, the car will travel fewer miles than kilometers on the same
gallon of gas. You can eliminate (C) and (D). Often, the answer that
you get if you set your proportion upside down (reverse the numerator
and denominator on one side) is a choice, and you can avoid falling

for this trap if you've already ruled out that answer. For example, $\dfrac{1.61}{1} = \dfrac{x \; miles}{28.5 \; kilometers}$ will give you $x = 45.88$, choice (D), which you've already ruled out. You would know in this case that you needed to double-check your proportion.

Quadratics and Polynomials

Multiplying Binomials

A binomial is an algebraic expression that is the sum or difference of two terms. For example, $x + 3$ is a binomial. To multiply two binomials, you need to use FOIL.

FOIL stands for First, Outer, Inner, Last.

Take a look at the following:

$$(x + 3)(x - 6) =$$

First: $(\underline{x} + 3)(\underline{x} - 6)$

Multiply the first term in one binomial by the first term in the other: $(x)(x) = x^2$

Outer: $(\underline{x} + 3)(x \; \underline{- \, 6})$

Multiply the outer terms, including the + or −: $(x)(-6) = -6x$

Inner: $(x \; \underline{+ \, 3})(\underline{x} - 6)$

Multiply the two inner terms, including the + or −: $(+3)(x) = +3x$

Last: $(x + 3)(x - 6)$

Multiply the second terms in each binomial: $(+3)(-6) = -18$

Finally, add up the terms and combine like terms:

$$x^2 - 6x + 3x - 18 = x^2 - 3x - 18$$

Factoring Quadratics

The product of the two binomials in the previous example is called a quadratic. A quadratic equation is an equation whose highest power is 2. You may recognize the standard form:

$$ax^2 + bx + c = 0.$$

Recall that a *coefficient* is a number in front of an x term, so a is the coefficient on x^2 and b is the coefficient on x. The c is the *constant term*.

Look at the example above again: $(x + 3)(x - 6) = x^2 - 3x - 18$. Notice that in the quadratic the b is the sum of the second terms in the binomials: $(+ 3)$ and $(- 6)$. The c is the product of the second terms in the binomials $(+ 3)$ and $(- 6)$. This is true for any quadratic in standard form in which $a = 1$.

Take a look at the following equation.

$$3x^2 + 6x = 45$$

First, subtract the 45 from both sides to put the equation into standard form:

$$3x^2 + 6x - 45 = 0$$

Since the coefficient on x^2 is a factor of both b and c, you can factor this term out first:

$$3(x^2 + 2x - 15) = 0$$

Now, to solve this equation, divide both sides by 3 then factor the $x^2 + 2x - 15$ into two *binomial factors*. Since $a = 1$, you need to find two factors of -15 that add to $+2$.

$$(x + 5)(x - 3) = 0$$

The last step is to set each binomial equal to 0.

$$(x + 5) = 0 \; ; x = -5$$
$$(x - 3) = 0; x = +3$$

The *solutions*, also known as *roots*, of this equation are $x = -5$, and $x = +3$. The roots will always have the opposite signs as the binomial factors.

Here are a few things to keep in mind when you are trying to find factors of a quadratic:

- If the c is positive, both factors will have the same sign as b, and therefore, both solutions will have opposite signs as b:

$x^2 + 7x + 12 = 0$ factors to $(x + 3)(x + 4) = 0$; solutions are $x = -3, x = -4$

$x^2 - 7x + 12 = 0$ factors to $(x - 3)(x - 4) = 0$; solutions are $x = 3, x = 4$

- If the c term is negative, the factors will have different signs:

$x^2 + x - 12 = 0$ factors to $(x - 3)(x + 4) = 0$; solutions are $x = 3, x = -4$

$x^2 - x - 12 = 0$ factors to $(x + 3)(x - 4) = 0$; solutions are $x = -3, x = 4$

There are also a few common quadratics that you want to familiarize yourself with:

- $(x + n)^2 = (x + n)(x + n) = x^2 + nx + nx + n^2 = x^2 + 2nx + n^2$

  Example: $(x + 4)(x + 4) = x^2 + 8x + 16$

- $(x - n)^2 = (x - n)(x - n) = x^2 - nx - nx + n^2 = x^2 - 2nx + n^2$

  Example: $(x - 4)(x - 4) = x^2 - 8x + 16$

- $(x - n)(x + n) = x^2 + nx - nx - n^2 = x^2 - n^2$

  Example: $(x + 4)(x - 4) = x^2 - 16$

This last one is called a *difference of squares*. This is the only time that the middle term will cancel out. Note that this means that $x^2 + 16$ is not a factorable equation (without using imaginary numbers (see page 288)).

Try the problems on the following page yourself.

Your Turn—Exercise 6.3

Use FOIL and Simplify:

1. $(x + 2)(x + 5) =$ _____

2. $(x - 2)(x - 5) =$ _____

3. $(2x + 3)(x - 4) =$ _____

Factor and Solve:

4. $x^2 + 13x - 48 = 0$ (_____)(_____) = 0 $x =$ ____; $x =$ ____

5. $x^2 - 1 = 0$ (_____)(_____) = 0 $x =$ ____; $x =$ ____

6. $6x^2 + 19x + 10 = 0$ (_____)(_____) = 0 $x =$ ____; $x =$ ____

Answers and Explanations to Exercise 6.3

1. FOIL: $x^2 + 5x + 2x + 10 = x^2 + 7x + 10$

2. FOIL: $x^2 - 5x - 2x + 10 = x^2 - 7x + 10$

3. FOIL: $2x^2 - 8x + 3x - 12 = 2x^2 - 5x - 12$

4. $(x + 16)(x - 3) = 0$ $x = -16$; $x = 3$

   If you got stuck on this one, try listing all of the factors of 48: 1, 48; 2, 24; 3, 16; 4, 12; 6, 8. Since the c is negative, you need one positive and one negative factor, and since b is positive, the bigger factor must be the positive one. Try your options now. $-1 + 48 \neq 13$, $-2 + 24 \neq 13$, $-3 + 16 = 13$. You can stop as soon as you find the pair that works.

5. $(x + 1)(x - 1) = 0$ $x = -1$; $x = 1$

   Since there was not a middle term ($b = 0$), this had to be a difference of squares.

6. $(3x + 2)(2x + 5) = 0$ $x = -\dfrac{2}{3}$; $x = -\dfrac{5}{2}$

   This one was a little trickier. When $a \neq 1$, you can use the ideas of FOIL in reverse to think of the factors, but you may have to try out a few possibilities. All the signs are positive, so there are not negatives in the factors. The product of the FIRST terms is $6x^2$, so this could be x and $6x$ or $2x$ and $3x$. The product of the LAST terms is 10, so this could be 1 and 10, or 2 and 5. Test out different combinations of these coefficients until you find one that works. Lastly, it's tempting to say the solutions are -2 and -5, but remember that the solutions are found by setting the factors to 0: $(3x + 2) = 0$, $3x = -2$, $x = -\dfrac{2}{3}$ and $(2x + 5) = 0$, $2x = -5$, $x = -\dfrac{5}{2}$.

Now, try to apply these skills to the following question.

12

$$x^2 - 9x + c = 0$$

If both of the solutions to the equation above are integers, which of the following is a possible value of c ?

A) -18

B)   7

C)   14

D)   22

Use the answer choices to help you. There are many possible values for c, but only one of these values is an answer choice. Try each choice and see if you can factor the equation. If the solutions are both integers, then the equation is factorable. Since the coefficient on x^2 is 1, remember that the constants in the binomial factors should have a sum of -9 and a product of c. Choice (A) is appealing because you might immediately think of the factors $(x - 6)$ and $(x - 3)$, but watch your signs. In order for c to be a negative value, these factors must have different signs; therefore, they do not have a sum of -9. The other factor pairs for 18 are ± 1, ± 18 and ± 2, ± 9. There is no way to get a sum of -9 with either of these pairs, so eliminate (A). Try (B). Since 7 is a prime number, this would mean the factors had to be $(x \pm 1)$ and $(x \pm 7)$, both the same sign. These will also not add to -9, so eliminate (B). In (C), the factors $(x - 2)$ and $(x - 7)$ work: $(x - 2)(x - 7)$ $= x^2 - 7x - 2x + 14 = x^2 - 9x + 14$. The answer is (C).

The Quadratic Formula

Unfortunately, some quadratic equations cannot be factored easily.

Take a look at the following question:

13

What are the solutions to $2x^2 - 3x - 4 = 0$?

A) $x = \dfrac{-3 \pm \sqrt{41}}{4}$

B) $x = \dfrac{-3 \pm \sqrt{23}}{2}$

C) $x = \dfrac{3 \pm \sqrt{41}}{4}$

D) $x = \dfrac{3 \pm \sqrt{23}}{4}$

This equation cannot be easily factored, so you will need to use the *Quadratic Formula*:

$$x = \frac{-b \pm \sqrt{b^2 - 4ac}}{2a}$$

In this formula the values of a, b, and c are the coefficients when the quadratic is written in standard form ($ax^2 + bx + c = 0$).

Plug $a = 2$, $b = -3$, and $c = -4$ into the equation above, and be careful with your negatives:

$$x = \frac{-(-3) \pm \sqrt{(-3)^2 - 4(2)(-4)}}{2(2)}$$

At this point you know that the value outside of the square root symbol on the numerator is + 3 not −3, so you can eliminate (A) and (B). Now simplify:

$$x = \frac{3 \pm \sqrt{9 - (-32)}}{4} = \frac{3 \pm \sqrt{9 + 32}}{4} = \frac{3 \pm \sqrt{41}}{4},$$

which matches (C).

HINT

When the question asks for the solutions to a quadratic, if the answers are integers or fractions, try to factor it. If the answer choices have square roots in them, you'll need the quadratic formula.

Adding and Subtracting Polynomials

Take a look at this question:

6

Which of the following expressions is equivalent to $(2x^2y - 3yx + 2y^2x) - (4y^2x + 4yx - 3x^2y)$?

A) $-2x^2y + yx + 5y^2x$

B) $5x^2y - 7yx - 2y^2x$

C) $-2x^2y + yx + 6y^2x$

D) $5x^2y - 7yx + 6y^2x$

Whenever a question asks you to find the difference or the sum of two polynomials, use POE heavily. Start with whichever piece is easiest for you, and eliminate as you go rather than trying to do the whole thing at once. Start by looking only at the terms with x^2y. In the first polynomial this is $2x^2y$, and in the second polynomial it is $-3x^2y$. Make sure to actually check the terms carefully because they may not be in the same order! Now subtract just these two terms: $2x^2y - (-3x^2y) = 5x^2y$. Eliminate (A) and (C) because they have the wrong coefficient on this term. Both (B) and (D) have the same middle term, so look at the y^2x terms. In the first polynomial you have $2y^2x$ and in the second you have $4y^2x$. When you subtract these two terms you get $2y^2x - 4y^2x = -2y^2x$. Eliminate (D). The answer is (B).

Exponents and Roots

In the expression x^a, x is called the base, and a is the exponent or power.

When you multiply two terms with the same base, you add the exponents:

$$x^a \times x^b = x^{a+b} \qquad\qquad x^3 \times x^4 = x^7$$

To divide two terms with the same base, you subtract the exponents:

$$\frac{x^a}{x^b} = x^{a-b} \qquad\qquad \frac{x^7}{x^3} = x^4$$

To raise an expression with an exponent to another power, you multiply the exponents:

$$(x^a)^b = x^{ab} \qquad\qquad (x^3)^4 = x^{12}$$

You'll also need to know that $x^{-a} = \dfrac{1}{x^a}$. For example $x^{-3} = \dfrac{1}{x^3}$.

Try to solve for n in each of the following:

1. $\dfrac{6x^6}{2x^2} = 3x^n$ $n = $ _____

2. $(x^{-2})^3 = \dfrac{1}{x^n}$ $n = $ _____

3. $(2x^{-3})^3 \times 2x^4 = 16x^n$ $n = $ _____

Answers:

1. You should divide the coefficients, but you need to subtract the exponents: $\left(\dfrac{6}{2}\right)(x^{6-2}) = 3x^4$; $n = 4$

2. Multiply the exponents: $(x^{-2})^3 = x^{-6}$, which is the same as $\dfrac{1}{x^6}$; $n = 6$

3. Simplify the first expression by multiplying the exponents. You must also raise the coefficient to the power of 3: $2^3(x^{-3\times3}) = 8x^{-9}$. Now, to multiply this by the second term, you need to multiply the coefficients and add the exponents: $(8 \times 2)(x^{-9+4}) = 16x^{-5}$; $n = -5$.

Roots

An expression that takes a root of a number is known as a *radical*.

Consider the following:

$$\sqrt[n]{x} = y$$

The symbol is called a *radical symbol*, the n is the *index* of the radical, and the x is the *radicand*. The radicand is whatever is under the radical symbol. In the expression above, y is the nth root of x, which means that $y^n = x$.

Radical expressions of the same index can be multiplied by multiplying the radicands. Similarly, they can be divided by dividing the radicands.

$$\sqrt[3]{x} \times \sqrt[3]{y} = \sqrt[3]{xy} \qquad\qquad \sqrt[3]{16} \times \sqrt[3]{4} = \sqrt[3]{64} = 4$$

$$\frac{\sqrt{x}}{\sqrt{y}} = \sqrt{\frac{x}{y}} \qquad\qquad \frac{\sqrt{72}}{\sqrt{2}} = \sqrt{36} = 6$$

Just as exponents must have the same base to be multiplied or divided, roots must have the same index to be multiplied.

Radicals *cannot* be added and subtracted, so $\sqrt{36} - \sqrt{9} \neq \sqrt{36 - 9}$.

The left side simplifies to 3, but the right side is $\sqrt{27}$.

Rational Exponents

Sometimes you will be given rational exponents. A rational exponent is an exponent in the form of a fraction, such as $x^{\frac{3}{4}}$. These may look scary, but they follow a simple rule. The numerator represents a power, and the denominator is a root. Therefore, $x^{\frac{3}{4}} = \sqrt[4]{x^3}$. You'll be expected to know how to convert between expressions with rational exponents and expressions with radicals.

Try the following questions.

1. Rewrite $x^{\frac{5}{2}}$ using a radical sign: _____

2. Rewrite $\sqrt[3]{x^2}$ using a rational exponent: _____

3. $\left(\sqrt[3]{x^5}\right)^2 = x^n$ $n =$ _____

Answers:

1. Raise x to the 5th power and take the 2nd root (which is just the square root): $\sqrt{x^5}$

2. x is raised to the 2nd power and then taken to the cube root, so the numerator is 2 and the denominator is 3: $x^{\frac{2}{3}}$.

3. First, rewrite the inside of the parentheses as a rational exponent: $\left(x^{\frac{5}{3}}\right)^2$ Multiply the exponents to get $x^{\frac{10}{3}}$; $n = \dfrac{10}{3}$.

Now, try these skills on a harder question:

8

Which of the following is equivalent to $25^{\frac{5}{4}}$?

A) $\sqrt{125}$

B) $5\sqrt{5}$

C) $25\sqrt{5}$

D) $25\sqrt{125}$

You could rewrite this as $\sqrt[4]{25^5}$, but it would not help you much since it is not an answer choice and you are unlikely to know the value of 25^5 without a calculator. Instead, try to rewrite this in terms that you do know. You can rewrite this expression as $\left(25^{\frac{4}{4}}\right)\left(25^{\frac{1}{4}}\right)$ since $\dfrac{4}{4} + \dfrac{1}{4} = \dfrac{5}{4}$. This simplifies to $25\left(25^{\frac{1}{4}}\right)$. Now, you can replace the 25 in the parentheses with 5^2 to get $25(5^2)^{\frac{1}{4}}$. You are raising an exponent

to a power, so multiply the exponents: $25\left(5^{\frac{2}{4}}\right) = 25\left(5^{\frac{1}{2}}\right) = 25\sqrt{5}$.

The answer is (C).

This is not the only way you could have gotten to this answer. You

could, for instance, have started by replacing 25 with 5^2 to get $(5^2)^{\frac{5}{4}}$,

and then multiplied the exponents to get $5^{\frac{10}{4}} = 5^{\frac{5}{2}} = 5^{\frac{4}{2}}\left(5^{\frac{1}{2}}\right)$

$= 5^2\left(\sqrt{5}\right) = 25\sqrt{5}$. There is no one correct way to solve questions

such as this one; as long as you follow the exponent rules in each

step, you will get to the same answer in the end.

If you get stuck, don't forget the power of estimation and POE. $25^{\frac{5}{4}}$

has to be bigger than 25 because $\frac{5}{4} > 1$. Eliminate (B). You can also

eliminate (A) because $5\sqrt{5}$ is clearly less than 5×5, so it is there-

fore less than 25. Now take a look at (C) and (D). Since $2^2 = 4$ and

$3^2 = 9$, $\sqrt{5}$ must be between 2 and 3, so (C) is a value between 50

and 75. This seems reasonable. Look at (D). Since $10^2 = 100$, the

$\sqrt{125}$ is a little more than 10, which means this value is greater than

250, which is too high. Choose (C).

Working with Radicals

Sometimes you will be given equations that have radical signs in them.

Take a look at the following question:

16

$$\sqrt{5x^2 - 29} - 4 = 0$$

If $x > 0$, what value of x is the solution to the equation above?

To solve an equation with a radical in it, you must first isolate the radical. Add 4 to both sides to get $\sqrt{5x^2 - 29} = 4$.

Now, you can get rid of the radical sign by squaring both sides:

$5x^2 - 29 = 4^2$, which simplifies to $5x^2 - 29 = 16$.

Add 29 to both sides: $5x^2 = 45$.

Then divide by 5 to get $x^2 = 9$.

Finally, take the square root of both sides to get $x = \pm 3$.

The question says that $x > 0$, so $x = 3$.

Try another:

9

$$\sqrt{x} + 2 = x$$

What is the solution set of the equation above?

A) {1, 2}

B) {4}

C) {1, 4}

D) {2}

Subtract 2 from both sides: $\sqrt{x} = x - 2$. Now square both sides. You may recall that $(x - 2)^2 = x^2 - 4x + 4$, but you can use FOIL if you do not. The equation is now $x = x^2 - 4x + 4$. Now you have a quadratic equation, so put it into standard form by subtracting x from both sides: $x^2 - 5x + 4 = 0$. This factors to $(x - 4)(x - 1) = 0$, so $x = 4$, or $x = 1$. You might be tempted to select (C) at this point. However, when solving equations with radicals, you always need to check that your answers actually work in the original equation because you may end up with an *extraneous solution*. An extraneous solution is a solution that you get when you solve the problem, but it does not actually work in the original. Try to put 1 in the original equation:

$\sqrt{1} + 2 = 1$. This statement is clearly not true. So 1 is not a possible solution.

$\sqrt{4} + 2 = 4$. This statement is true, so the answer is 4, (B).

Of course one way to avoid falling into extraneous solution traps is to use Plugging In the Answers to solve radical questions that are multiple choice. You could try $x = 1$ first because it's in two answers, and once you discovered that it did not work, you could eliminate (A) and (C). Then, you would try 4 and since it works, choose (B).

Your Turn—Exercise 6.4

8

$$\sqrt{3 - x} = x - 3$$

What is the solution set of the equation above?

A) {2}

B) {3}

C) {2,3}

D) {1, 6}

16

If $\sqrt[3]{x^5} \times \sqrt[4]{x} = x^{\frac{n}{12}}$, what is the value of n ?

6

If $\dfrac{2^{n^2}}{2^{m^2}} = 8$ and $n - m = 3$, what is the value of $n + m$?

A) 1

B) 2

C) 5

D) 11

7

A typical race car is traveling at its maximum speed along a straight section of track. The distance it covers in 1 second is equal to the length of a football field, which is 120 yards or 360 feet. What is the race car's maximum speed, in miles per hour? (1 mile = 5,280 feet)

A) 27

B) 82

C) 245

D) 528

5

If $7x + 3 = -x^2$, what are the values of x ?

A) $\dfrac{-7 \pm \sqrt{61}}{-2}$

B) $\dfrac{-7 \pm \sqrt{37}}{2}$

C) $\dfrac{-3 \pm \sqrt{-19}}{14}$

D) $\dfrac{3 \pm \sqrt{37}}{2}$

For more free content, visit PrincetonReview.com

2

Which of the following is equivalent to
$(2x - 3)(x + 4)$?

A) $2x^2 + 5x - 12$

B) $2x^2 + x - 12$

C) $2x^2 + 11x + 12$

D) $3x + 1$

Answers and Explanations to Exercise 6.4

8. **B** Plugging In the Answers is probably the easiest and fastest way to approach this problem. Since 2 and 3 are both in two answers, start with one of these. Using $x = 2$ gives you $\sqrt{1} = -1$. This is not true, so eliminate (A) and (C). Now check $x = 3$. This gives you $0 = 0$, so the answer must include 3. Choose (B). If you had chosen to solve this problem by squaring both sides, you would get both 2 and 3 as solutions, but don't forget to check for extraneous solutions. Since 2 does not work when you plug it back into the original equation, it is an extraneous solution.

16. **23** First, rewrite each term with rational exponents: $\left(x^{\frac{5}{3}}\right) \times \left(x^{\frac{1}{4}}\right)$. Since you are multiplying the terms, you need to add the exponents. You can do this by using the bowtie method: $\dfrac{5}{3} + \dfrac{1}{4} = \dfrac{4(5) + 1(3)}{3(4)} = \dfrac{23}{12}$. The value of $\dfrac{n}{12} = \dfrac{23}{12}$, so $n = 23$.

6. **A** You are dividing two terms with the same base, so subtract the exponents: $2^{n^2 - m^2} = 8$. You can also rewrite 8 as 2^3 to get $2^{n^2 - m^2} = 2^3$. This means that $n^2 - m^2 = 3$. You can then rewrite $n^2 - m^2$ as $(n - m)(n + m)$. The question already states that $n - m = 3$, so $3(n + m) = 3$ and $n + m = 1$.

7. **C** The question gives the distance traveled in 1 second in both yards and feet. Since the other information in the problem regards feet per mile, focus on the measurement in feet. There are 60 seconds in a minute, and in each

the car travels 360 feet, so it travels 360 feet × 60 seconds = 21,600 feet in one minute. There are 60 minutes in an hour, so multiply by 60 again to find that it travels at 1,296,000 feet per hour. Now set up a proportion to find out how many miles that would be:

$$\frac{1 \text{ } mile}{5,280 \text{ } feet} = \frac{x}{1,296,000 \text{ } feet}$$

Cross-multiply and solve for x to find that the car's speed is about 245 miles per hour.

5. **B** To solve this quadratic equation, first set the equation equal to zero by adding x^2 to both sides; you get $x^2 + 7x + 3 = 0$. This won't factor nicely; 3 only has integer factors 1 and 3, which don't add up to 7. Furthermore, the answer choices give away that the result isn't pretty. In this case, use the quadratic formula: $x = \dfrac{-b \pm \sqrt{b^2 - 4ac}}{2a}$, when the equation is in the form $ax^2 + bx + c$. In this equation, $a = 1$, $b = 7$, and $c = 3$. Plug in these values and solve:

$$x = \frac{-7 \pm \sqrt{7^2 - 4(1)(3)}}{2(1)}$$

$$x = \frac{-7 \pm \sqrt{49 - 12}}{2}$$

$$x = \frac{-7 \pm \sqrt{37}}{2}$$

This is (B).

2. **A** One approach is to use the FOIL technique: First, Outer, Inner, Last. In other words, you multiply the first terms, then the outside terms, then the inside terms, and then the last terms. Finally, add the products. Be careful with negatives:

$(2x)(x) = 2x^2$

$(2x)(4) = 8x$

$(-3)(x) = -3x$

$(-3)(4) = -12$

$2x^2 + 8x + (-3x) + (-12) = 2x^2 + 5x - 12$

This is (A).

Alternatively, you can plug in. Make $x = 2$, so $[2(2) - 3](2 + 4)$ $= (4 - 3)(2 + 4) = (1)(6) = 6$. This is your target. Make $x = 2$ in each answer choice. The only choice that equals 6 when $x = 2$ is (A).

Step 7: Charts and Data

On the test, you'll be given data in a variety of forms and asked a series of questions about it. The most important thing to keep in mind on all data questions is to read the titles, axes labels, legends, and units carefully before you begin solving questions. Beyond that, you should be familiar with the different types of data and questions you might see. This chapter offers an overview of the most common forms of data on the test.

Bar Graph

A bar graph is a graph that shows the distribution of data. The bar graph below shows the distribution of the number of hours students in a class chose to spend at a particular exhibit on a field trip to a museum.

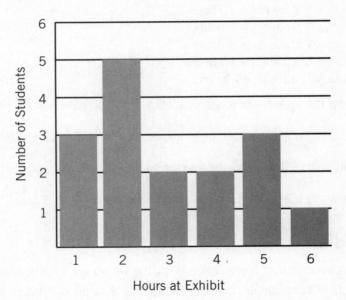

On the SAT you may be asked to find the mean, median, mode, or range of the data.

Mean

The terms *mean*, *arithmetic mean*, and *average* all mean the same thing.

$$\text{Mean} = \frac{\text{total sum of values}}{\text{number of values}}$$

To solve for the mean number of hours the students spent at the museum, you first need to find the total sum of hours spent at the museum. Do this one piece at a time:

1 hour × 3 students = 3 hours
2 hours × 5 students = 10 hours
3 hours × 2 students = 6 hours
4 hours × 2 students = 8 hours
5 hours × 3 students = 15 hours
6 hours × 1 student = 6 hours

Add up the total hours to get 3 + 10 + 6 + 8 + 15 + 6 = 48 hours.

Now, add up the number of students: 3 + 5 + 2 + 2 + 3 + 1 = 16 students. The mean, or average, number of hours spent at the museum by the students in the class is therefore $\frac{48}{16}$ = 3 hours.

Median

The *median* is the middle value when the values are listed in numerical order. For example, the median of {1, 2, 3, 4, 5} is 3. When there is an even number of terms in a list, the median is the average of the middle two terms. For example, the median of {1, 2, 3, 4, 5, 6} = $\frac{3 + 4}{2}$ = 3.5.

It can be tempting to look at the bar graph above and say that the median is 3.5 because this is the median of {1, 2, 3, 4, 5, 6}, but you have to take into account the fact that there are multiple students for most of these values. The actual list of values looks like this:

{1, 1, 1, 2, 2, 2, 2, 2, 3, 3, 4, 4, 5, 5, 5, 6}

This is a lot to write out, and often bar graphs will have many more than 16 total terms. Instead of writing out all the terms, use the following formula to determine which term represents the median.

Median term = $\frac{n + 1}{2}$ when n = the total number of terms.

This means that the median term of 16 students is $\frac{16 + 1}{2}$. This does not mean that the median is 8.5, but rather that the median is the average of the 8th term and the 9th term. Since you have an even number of students, the median has to be the average of two terms.

Now look back at the bar graph. There are 3 students that spent 1 hour and 5 students that spent 2 hours, so a total of 8 students spent 2 hours or less at the museum. This means that the 8th term is 2 and the 9th term is 3. Therefore, the median of the data in the bar graph is the average of 2 and 3: $\frac{2 + 3}{2} = \frac{5}{2}$ = 2.5 hours.

Mode

The mode of a data set is the number that occurs most frequently. The mode is easy to find in a bar graph. Since there were more students that spent 2 hours in the exhibit than any of the other number of hours, the mode number of hours in the exhibit is 2 hours. Note that not all sets of data have a mode. For instance, the list {1, 2, 2, 3, 3, 4, 5} does not have a mode because both 2 and 3 appear twice and nothing appears more than twice.

Range

The range of a set of data is the difference between the highest value and the lowest value. You might be tempted to say that the range is 6 because the highest value is 6, but notice that not all bar graphs start at zero. The lowest value is 1, so the range is $6 - 1 = 5$.

Frequency Table

It's possible that you may see a frequency table on the test. A frequency table is another way to represent the same data as a bar graph. The table below represents the same information as the bar graph above.

Number of Hours	Number of Students
1	3
2	5
3	2
4	2
5	3
6	1

You can use all of the same techniques to solve for the mean, median, mode, and range of a frequency table. In fact, the mean is even easier to find because the values are already arranged for you. You can add a column to the right side to represent the sum of each set of values and a row at the bottom to find the total number of students and total number of hours.

Number of Hours	Number of Students	Hours × Students
1	3	3
2	5	10
3	2	6
4	2	8
5	3	15
6	1	6
	Total students: 16	Total Hours: 48

Try to find the mean, median, mode, and range of this data set yourself.

Your Turn—Exercise 7.1

The bar graph below shows the distribution of the number of absences for the students in a history class.

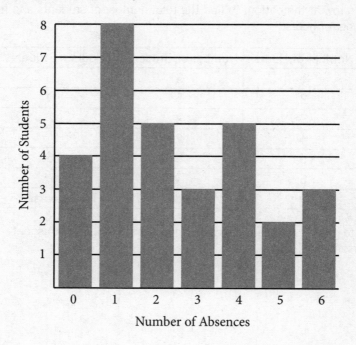

1. Mean number of absences =   _____

2. Median number of absences =   _____

3. Mode of absences =   _____

4. Range of absences =   _____

Answers and Explanations to Exercise 7.1

1. Mean: Find the number of students and the total absences:

$$0 \times 4 = 0$$
$$1 \times 8 = 8$$
$$2 \times 5 = 10$$
$$3 \times 3 = 9$$
$$4 \times 5 = 20$$
$$5 \times 2 = 10$$
$$6 \times 3 = 18$$

The total number of students is 30, and the total number of absences is 75. The mean is $\dfrac{total\ absences}{total\ students} = \dfrac{75}{30} = 2.5$ absences.

2. Median: There are 30 students, so the median term is the average of the 15th and 16th terms $\left(\dfrac{31}{2} = 15.5 \right)$. There are 4 students with 0 absences and 8 students with 1 absence for a total of 12 students with fewer than 2 absences. Since the next 5 students have 2 absences, both the 15th and 16th students have 2 absences. The median is 2.

3. Mode: There are a total of 8 students with 1 absence. This frequency is higher than any of the other values, so the mode is 1.

4. Range: The greatest number of absences is 6 and the least number of absences is 0, so the range is $6 - 0 = 6$.

Tables

Always read the blurb located above or below any table data that explains what the data means before you start solving any questions.

	Candidate A	Candidate B	Candidate C	Total
Virginia	7,713	9,244	3,377	20,334
Maryland	4,320	4,253	1,025	9,598
Delaware	1,760	1,963	487	4,210
Pennsylvania	4,410	5,686	2,392	12,488
Total	18,203	21,146	7,281	46,630

A news station conducted exit polls after the primaries for four states. Participants were asked to indicate which of the three candidates on the ballot they voted for. The results of the survey are shown above.

Percents

Percent means out of 100, so 20 percent of x can be written in fractional form as $\frac{20}{100}$ x or in decimal form as 0.20x.

Take a look at the following questions:

31

Based on the table above, approximately what percent of the voters surveyed in Virginia voted for Candidate C? (Round your answer to the nearest tenth.)

The question can be written as $\dfrac{x}{100} = \dfrac{\textit{votes for C in Virginia}}{\textit{voters surveyed in Virginia}}$,

which means that $x = \dfrac{\textit{votes for C in Virginia}}{\textit{voters surveyed in Virginia}} \times 100$.

Find the values of these numbers in the table to get $x = \dfrac{3{,}377}{20{,}334} \times 100$ ≈ 16.7.

 32

> If exactly 3% of the voters that voted in the primary in Virginia were surveyed, how many thousands of voters voted in this primary in Virginia, rounded to the nearest thousand?

You can rewrite this as $\dfrac{3}{100}x = \textit{surveyed voters}$ or $0.03x = \textit{surveyed}$ *voters*. The table indicates that 20,334 voters were surveyed in Virginia, so this equation becomes $0.03x = 20{,}334$. Divide both sides by 0.03 to get $x = 677{,}800$. Because the question asks for how many thousands of voters voted, rounded to the nearest thousand, the answer is 678.

Crash Course for the SAT

Probability

Probability is $\dfrac{\textit{outcomes that fit the requirement}}{\textit{total possible outcomes}}$. Note that probability must be between 0 and 1 because the numerator, outcomes that fit the requirement, cannot possibly be more than the total possible outcomes.

Take a look at this question. Although we've based the next few questions on the same table as questions 31 and 32 above, the real SAT will not repeat the same table for multiple sets, and sets will only have 2–3 questions.

11

If a survey participant is selected at random, what is the approximate probability that he is either from Virginia or Delaware?

A) 0.36

B) 0.44

C) 0.53

D) 0.64

The numerator is the number of outcomes that fit the requirement, which is all of the voters from Virginia and all the voters from Delaware: 20,334 + 4,210 = 24,544. The question says a survey participant is selected at random, so the possible outcomes are the total possible voters in the survey, 46,630. Therefore, the probability is $\dfrac{24,544}{46,630}$, which is approximately 0.53, (C).

182   For more free content, visit PrincetonReview.com

Be careful though. The denominator is often a subset of the total. Consider the following question:

12

> If a survey participant that voted for
> Candidate B is selected at random, what is
> the probability that the selected participant
> is from Virginia?
>
> A) 0.20
>
> B) 0.44
>
> C) 0.53
>
> D) 0.96

This time the question specified that the participant was randomly selected from the participants that voted for Candidate B, so the total possible outcomes in the denominator is the total number of participants that voted for Candidate B rather than the total number of participants. In the numerator, the outcomes that fit the requirement are the participants in Virginia that voted for Candidate B: 9,244. The probability is $\frac{9,244}{21,146} \approx 0.44$, which is (B).

Ratios

A *ratio* is similar to a fraction, but instead of a part to whole relationship, it is a part to part relationship. For example, the fraction of votes for Candidate A in Virginia is $\frac{7,713}{20,334}$, but the *ratio* of votes for Candidate A to votes for Candidate B is $\frac{votes\ for\ A}{votes\ for\ B} = \frac{7,713}{9,244}$. This ratio can also be written in the equivalent form 7,713: 9,244. Consider the following question:

13

Based on the survey data, for which state is the ratio of votes for Candidate B to votes for Candidate C closest to the ratio of the total votes for Candidate B to total votes for Candidate C for all of the survey participants in the four states?

A) Virginia

B) Maryland

C) Delaware

D) Pennsylvania

Start by determining the total ratio for the region: $\dfrac{\textit{total votes for B}}{\textit{total votes for C}} =$

$\dfrac{21{,}146}{7{,}281} \approx 2.90$.

Then find the ratio of for each individual state:

Virginia $= \dfrac{9{,}244}{3{,}377} \approx 2.73$

Maryland $= \dfrac{4{,}253}{1{,}025} \approx 4.15$

Delaware $= \dfrac{1{,}963}{487} \approx 4.03$

Pennsylvania $= \dfrac{5{,}686}{2{,}392} \approx 2.38$

2.73 is closer to 2.90 than any of the other values, so the answer is Virginia. If the question had asked for the greatest ratio, the answer would be Maryland, and if it had asked for the least ratio, the answer would be Pennsylvania.

Determining Population Characteristics from Sample Data

Sometimes you will be asked to estimate characteristics about a population based on table data about a sample from the population.

Take a look at this question:

14

If a total of 898,400 people voted in the primary in Pennsylvania, which of the following is the best approximation of the number of total votes cast for Candidate C in Pennsylvania?

A)   173,083

B)   140,280

C)   46,086

D)   19,065

Use proportions to solve questions like this: $\dfrac{total\ survey\ votes\ in\ PA}{total\ actual\ votes\ in\ PA} =$

$\dfrac{survey\ votes\ for\ C\ in\ PA}{actual\ votes\ for\ C\ in\ PA}$, which is $\dfrac{12,488}{898,400} = \dfrac{2,392}{x}$. Cross-

multiply to get $12,488x = 2,392(898,400)$; $x \approx 173,083$, (A).

Try to answer the following questions using the data given on the next page.

For more free content, visit PrincetonReview.com

Your Turn—Exercise 7.2

Questions 15–18 refer to the following information.

	Spanish	German	French	Total
Juniors	87	12	24	123
Seniors	95	15	42	152
Total	182	27	66	275

The table above shows the number of students enrolled in each of the foreign languages offered at a particular school.

15

Which of the following groups makes up approximately 9% of the juniors and seniors enrolled in a foreign language at this school?

A) Total students taking German

B) Juniors taking French

C) Juniors taking German

D) Seniors taking French

16

Assume that the proportion of students in each grade enrolled in each foreign language at this school is representative of the entire school system. If there are 3,000 total juniors enrolled in foreign language in the school system, which of the following is the closest approximation of the number of juniors who take Spanish in the school system?

A)   950

B)   1,875

C)   1,986

D)   2,122

17

Based on the data above, which of the following ratios is the greatest?

A)   Juniors taking French to seniors taking French

B)   Juniors taking Spanish to seniors taking Spanish

C)   Students taking French to students taking German

D)   Seniors taking German to juniors taking German

If one of the students who is enrolled in French is selected at random, what is the approximate probability that the student is a senior?

A) $\dfrac{42}{66}$

B) $\dfrac{42}{152}$

C) $\dfrac{42}{276}$

D) $\dfrac{24}{42}$

Answers and Explanations to Exercise 7.2

15. **B** To tackle this question, use the chart to identify the total number of students who take a foreign language, which is 275. Next, use the answer choices to locate the appropriate data and determine which is closest to 9%. In (A), the total number of students taking German is 27, so $\frac{27}{275} \times 100$ ≈ 9.8%. This is close, but would round to 10%, so keep checking. In (B), the number of juniors taking French is 24, so $\frac{24}{275} \times 100$ ≈ 8.7%. This is approximately 9%. You can see that neither (C) nor (D) is close to this value, so the correct answer is (B).

Alternatively, you could find 9% of 275 with the formula 0.09(275) = 24.75. Of the answer choices, the number of juniors taking French, 24, is closest to this value.

16. **D** To tackle this question, set up a proportion to relate the given values. The proportion needs to relate the data for the school to the data for the entire school system. It can be set up like this:

$$\frac{\text{Total juniors at high school in study}}{\text{Total juniors in entire school system}} = \frac{\text{Juniors in Spanish at high school in study}}{\text{Juniors in Spanish in the school system}}$$

For more free content, visit <u>PrincetonReview.com</u>

Gather the relevant numbers from the table and plug them into the proportion:

$$\frac{123}{3,000} = \frac{87}{x}$$

$$123x = 87 \times 3,000$$

$$123x = 261,000$$

$$x \approx 2,122$$

The correct answer is (D).

17. **C** Determine the ratios described in each answer by identifying the relevant data from the chart provided. In (A), the number of juniors taking French and the number of seniors taking French are 24 and 42, respectively. The ratio is $\frac{24}{42} \approx 0.57$. In (B), the ratio of juniors taking Spanish to seniors taking Spanish is $\frac{87}{95} \approx 0.92$, which is greater, so eliminate (A). In (C), the ratio of students taking French to students taking German is $\frac{66}{27} \approx 2.44$, which is greater, so eliminate (B). In (D), the ratio of seniors taking German to juniors taking German is $\frac{15}{12} = 1.25$. This is not greater than (C), so eliminate (D). The correct answer is (C).

18. **A** Recall that probability is defined as $\dfrac{outcomes\ that\ fit\ the\ requirement}{total\ possible\ outcomes}$. In this case, the probability is $\dfrac{Seniors\ who\ take\ French}{Total\ number\ of\ students\ who\ take\ French}$.

Plug the numbers from the provided chart in to find the probability: $\dfrac{42}{66}$. The correct answer is (A).

Scatterplot

A *scatterplot* is a graph that shows the relationship between two variables.

Take a look at the data below:

A researcher conducts a study to determine how sleep affects cognitive speed. He records the amount of sleep each participant gets one night and then measures the amount of time it takes to complete a task the following morning. The results are shown in the scatterplot below.

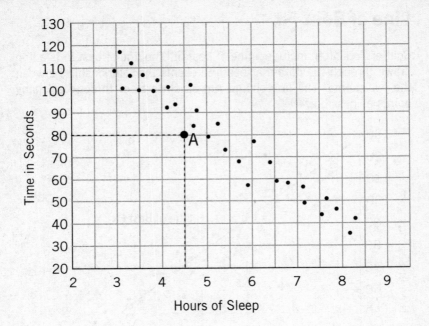

Each dot in a scatterplot represents a data point. For example, the point marked A represents a participant who received 4.5 hours of sleep and took 80 seconds to complete the task.

Line of Best Fit

Scatterplots often include a line of best fit. The line of best fit is a line drawn through the data that best represents the relationship between the two points. The line should run as close to or through as many points as possible.

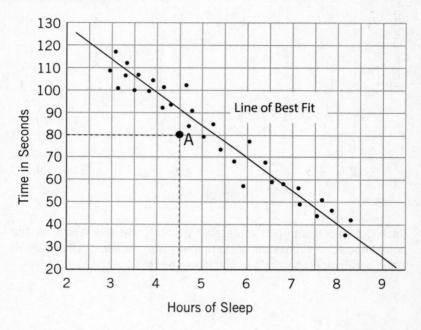

This line of best fit can be used to estimate values.

Consider the following:

5

Based on the line of best fit, approximately how long would the researcher predict that it would take a person to complete the task after 4.5 hours of sleep the previous night?

A) 80 seconds

B) 92 seconds

C) 97 seconds

D) 104 seconds

Even though there is a data point that indicates that a participant who slept 4.5 hours of sleep took 80 seconds to complete the task, the question asks what the *line of best fit* would predict. At 4.5 hours of sleep, the line of best fit has a value of just over 90 seconds. The answer is (B).

Percent Change

It's possible that the question may ask you about the difference between actual values and predicted values.

Take a look at this question:

24

The participant that had exactly 4.5 hours of sleep took approximately what percent less time to complete the task than the value predicted by the line of best fit?

A) 13%

B) 15%

C) 17%

D) 20%

The formula for percent change is $\dfrac{difference}{original} \times 100$. Be careful about which value you put in the denominator. Sometimes you can use the language of the question to help you. If the question states *percent decrease* or *percent less*, then the original is the larger value. If the question states *percent increase* or *percent more*, then the original is the smaller value.

In the previous question, you already determined that the predicted time for a person that got 4.5 hours of sleep is 92 seconds. You also know that the participant that got 4.5 hours of sleep took 80 seconds to complete the task. The original is 92 seconds because the question asks for the percent decrease from the predicted value. The formula

For more free content, visit PrincetonReview.com

therefore becomes $\dfrac{92 - 80}{92} \times 100$, which simplifies to $\dfrac{12}{92} \times 100$, or approximately 13%.

Equation for the Line of Best Fit

In addition to determining predicted values based on the line of best fit, you'll need to know how to write the equation for one:

25

Which of the following could be the equation of the line of best fit for the scatterplot above?

A) $y = 15x + 115$

B) $y = 115 - 10x$

C) $y = 10x + 150$

D) $y = 160 - 15x$

Use the same concepts you learned in the previous chapter. The coefficient on the variable should be the rate of change, i.e. how much the value increases or decreases for each additional unit of sleep. Since the time required to complete the task decreases as the amount of sleep increases, you need the coefficient to be negative. You can eliminate (A) and (C). You have only two possible answers, so the easiest way to tackle this is to pick a point somewhere in the middle of the line and see which equation works with the coordinates of that point. At 6 hours, (B) would give you $y = 115 - 10(6) = 55$. However, the line of best fit has a value of 70 at 6 hours, so eliminate (B) and choose (D). Choice (D) gives you $y = 160 - 15(6) = 160 - 90 = 70$.

Your Turn—Exercise 7.3

Questions 20–23 refer to the following information.

The scatterplot below shows the number of hours students in a class studied and their scores on a particular test.

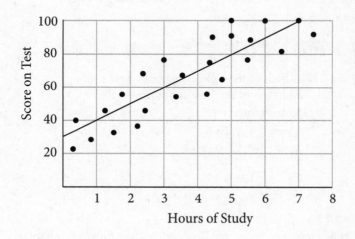

20

Based on the data above, which of the following statements is true?

A) The student who studied the most scored the highest on the test.

B) The lowest grade on the test was a 30.

C) According to the line of best fit, the predicted score for a student who studied for 4 hours is approximately 70.

D) The range of scores on the test was approximately 70.

For more free content, visit PrincetonReview.com

21

Which of the following is the equation for the line of best fit in the scatterplot above?

A) $y = 10x + 30$

B) $y = 30x + 10$

C) $y = 7x + 30$

D) $y = 100 - 10x$

22

The student who studied for exactly 3 hours scored approximately what percent higher on the test than predicted by the line of best fit?

A) 20%

B) 25%

C) 33%

D) 60%

23

How many students scored below the score predicted by the line of best fit based on the number of hours they studied?

A) 10

B) 11

C) 12

D) 13

Answers and Explanations to Exercise 7.3

20. **C**   Compare the statements in the answer choices to the provided scatterplot. In (A), though this may seem true based on the general trend, the student who spent the most time studying, 7.5 hours, did not receive the highest score. In (B), the line of best fit has an intercept at approximately 30, but the lowest grade according to the data is around 20. In (C), according to the line of best fit, at 4 hours the score is approximately 70, so keep it. In (D), recall that the range is the difference between the highest value and the lowest value. In this case, the highest is 100 and the lowest is about 20 making the range $100 - 20 = 80$. The correct answer is (C).

21. **A**   Since the score on the test increases as the hours spent studying increases, the coefficient in the equation needs to be positive, so (D) can be eliminated. Choose a coordinate on the line of best fit. At 4 hours of studying, the line of best fits says the score is 70. Plug 4 into (A) to see if $y = 70$: $10(4) + 30 = 70$, so keep it and check the remaining answer choices to be sure. In (B), $30(4) + 10 = 130$ and in (D), $7(4) + 30 = 58$. The correct answer is (A).

22. **C**   Percent change is defined as $\dfrac{difference}{original} \times 100$. The question states *percent higher,* so the original number will be the smaller number. The relevant data points at 3 hours are 60 from the line of best fit and 80 from the scatterplot. Calculate the percent change: $\dfrac{80 - 60}{60} \times 100 = \dfrac{20}{60} \times 100 \approx$ 33%. The correct answer is (C).

For more free content, visit <u>PrincetonReview.com</u>

23. **B**   To determine the number of students who scored below the predicted value, carefully count the number of points that appear below the line of best fit. In this case, there are 11 data points below the line. The correct answer is (B).

POE on Charts and Data

Questions related to graphs often come down to Process of Elimination. Make sure you check the units and labels carefully and eliminate any answer that does not match what you see in the graph.

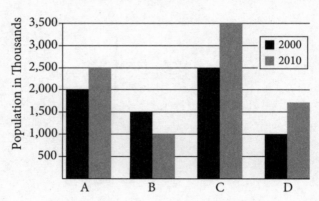

Population by Region in 2000 and 2010

The bar graph above shows the populations in four metropolitan regions in 2000 and 2010. Based on the information shown, which of the following statements is true?

A) The population of Region C increased by approximately 1,000 between 2000 and 2010.

B) The population of Region B increased by approximately 500,000 between 2000 and 2010.

C) Of the four regions shown, Region D had the greatest percent increase in population between 2000 and 2010.

D) Of the regions shown, Region D had the lowest population in 2010.

Before you jump into the answers, pay attention to the axes labels. The *y*-axis says that the population is given in thousands, so 500 would mean a population of 500,000. Read the legend as well. The darker shaded bars represent the population in 2000, and the lighter shaded bars represent the population in 2010. Now, check the answers one at a time. The statement in (A) is not true because the *y*-axis represents thousands, so an increase of 1,000 along the axis is actually an increase of 1,000,000 in population. The statement in (B) is not true either because the population of Region B actually decreases between 2000 and 2010. The statement in (C) says Region D had the greatest percent increase in population. You might be tempted to eliminate this because Region C increased by more, but you have to calculate the *percent increase* not the actual increase. You do not need to check Region B because its population decreased, but check each of the others. The percent increase for Region A is $\frac{difference}{original} \times 100 = \frac{500}{2,000} \times 100 = 25\%$. The percent increase for Region C is $\frac{1,000}{2,500} \times 100 = 40\%$, and the percent increase for Region D is $\frac{750}{1,000} \times 100 = 75\%$. Region D has the greatest percent increase, so this statement is true. Check the statement in (D) just to be sure. This is not true, because Region D has the lowest population in 2000, but Region B has the lowest population in 2010. The answer is (C).

Try the question on the following page.

A financial advisor tracks the stock price per share for a company over the course of a 30-day month. The data are graphed on the axes below with the time in days since the beginning of the month on the x-axis and the stock price per share on the y-axis.

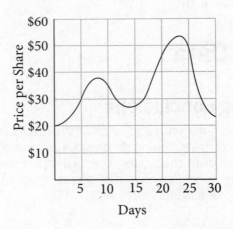

Based on the graph, which of the following statements is true?

A)   The stock's lowest price is at the end of the month.

B)   The stock reaches its highest price around the 23rd day.

C)   The stock price increases steadily for the first 10 days.

D)   The x-intercept represents the stock's value at the beginning of the month.

Begin by evaluating each of the statements in the answers compared to the collected data. In (A), the stock price appears to dip to its lowest at month's end, but at the beginning of the month it actually has a lower value, so eliminate this choice. In (B), at around day 23, the graph appears to achieve its highest point, so keep it for now. In (C), during the first 10 days, the stock increases and then decreases as it approaches the 10th day, so eliminate this choice. In (D), the y-intercept, not the x-intercept, would indicate the value of the stock at the beginning of the month (or at Day 0), so eliminate this choice. The correct answer is (B).

Survey Data

Supporting Conclusions

When a question gives you survey data or the results of a study and asks you which of the following conclusions is most supported, use POE heavily. You want the answer that makes the least number of assumptions. Be wary of answers that generalize to a broader set of people than the participants in the study.

Take a look at this question:

17

A city council is trying to determine resident support for a proposal to build a new football stadium for the local team. It conducts a survey of 50 people at a tailgate party in the parking lot before a home game, and 74% of the survey respondents say that they support the proposal to build a new stadium. Which of the following conclusions is most supported by the survey data?

A) The majority of city residents will be willing to support a tax increase to build the new stadium.

B) The proposal will pass if it is put on the ballot at the next election.

C) The majority of local football fans support the proposal.

D) The majority of local fans that attend games likely support the proposal.

Start with (A). You can eliminate this because the question makes no mention of a tax increase, so it is not supported by the data. Choice (B) is a little better than (A), but it still seems too strong to conclude that it will pass based only on a small survey at a football game. Choice (C) narrows the focus down to football fans, so this is more supported by the data than (B). Choice (D) is even closer to the survey data. The survey was given at a tailgate party, so the people surveyed are the fans that attend games. This is the best answer because it doesn't make any assumptions about any population other than the one surveyed.

Potential Flaws and How to Improve

You may be asked to determine a flaw in the experimental design, or how to improve a study. There are two main things to consider: sample size and representative samples.

If the survey asked only 50 people and the city has 200,000 residents, then it is difficult to draw many conclusions about the residents of the city based on such a small proportion of the residents. However, the even bigger problem is the sample selection. Even if the survey were expanded to 1,000 people, if it was still done at a tailgate party, then the results would not be appropriate for the city council to draw conclusions about resident support for the proposal because of potential bias. The sample is not likely to be a representative sample of the city population since the survey was conducted at a party for a football game. The results are skewed because the participants have a greater interest in the football team and its stadium than the population of the city as a whole.

In order to draw conclusions about the overall population from a sample, you need the sample to be representative of the population as a whole. Participants that are "randomly selected" are often the best way to gather a representative sample. A phone survey of 1,000 randomly selected residents would provide a better measure of the overall support for the stadium by city residents because there is no particular reason why this group would be biased for or against the stadium.

For more free content, visit PrincetonReview.com

Try this one yourself:

A drug company is testing a new drug, HairGro, to treat premature balding in men. The company randomly selected a sample of 500 men that were exhibiting hair loss between the ages of 18 and 35. Half of these participants were randomly selected to receive the treatment, and the other half received a placebo. The participants that received the drug reported significantly more hair growth than the participants that received the placebo. Which of the following conclusions is most supported by this data?

A) HairGro leads to thicker, fuller hair.

B) HairGro causes hair to grow significantly faster.

C) HairGro is the most effective treatment for hair loss in men suffering from premature hair loss.

D) HairGro likely improves hair growth in men suffering from premature balding.

Notice that the study used a randomly selected sample and has an adequate sample size, so the experimental design is well set up to test the drug's effectiveness at treating hair loss in prematurely balding men. However, you still need to select an answer that does not generalize any further than this. Choices (A) and (B) talk about the quality and speed of the hair growth, but no specifics were given about these things, so you can eliminate (A) and (B). Between (C) and (D), (D) is a better answer because there is no information given about the effectiveness of any other treatments. Choice (D) makes the least assumptions, and therefore is the conclusion that is most supported.

Step 8: Functions

Function Notation

A function is a set of operations that transforms one variable, the input, into another, the output. Often the input is referred to as x and the output is referred to as y. For example, $y = 4x + 3$ is a function in which x is the input and y is the output. Functions can also be written in function notation: $f(x) = 4x + 3$. In function notation, the output is the value of $f(x)$, and the input is the x. Function notation can use a variety of letters.

For instance, $g(n) = 4n + 3$ represents the same function as $f(x) = 4x + 3$. The input for any function in function notation is the value inside the parentheses.

Take a look at the following:

16

If $f(x) = 3x^2 - 2$, what is the value of $f(2)$?

The value inside the parentheses is 2, so this is the input. The only thing you need to do to solve this is to replace the x with the value 2: $f(2) = 3(2)^2 - 2 = 12 - 2 = 10$. The output, $f(2)$, of this function is 10.

Sometimes you will be given a set of input and output values and asked to find the function that fits them:

6

x	g(x)
0	−7
1	−4
2	−1
3	2

The table above shows some values of the linear function g. Which of the following defines g?

A) x − 7

B) x − 5

C) 2x − 5

D) 3x − 7

You can use Plugging In on this question. Plug x = 0 into the answer choices. The correct function will give you an output of −7. Choice (A) works, but make sure to check all of the answers. Choice (B) and (C) give you an output of −5 when x = 0, so eliminate these. Choice (D) also gives you −7, so keep it. Pick another value and try (A) and (D) again. When you plug x = 1 into x − 7 you get −6, but the table indicates that the value is −4, so eliminate (A). If you want to double check (D), you get 3x − 7 = 3(1) − 7 = −4. This works, so (D) is the answer.

Take a look at this one:

7

$$g(x) = \frac{2}{3}x + c$$

In the function above, c is a constant. If $g(9) = 3$, what is the value of $g(-6)$?

A) -7

B) -3

C) 2

D) 3

You need to solve for the value of c first. You can do this by substituting $x = 9$ and $g(x) = 3$ into the original function: $3 = \frac{2}{3}(9) + c$. This simplifies to $3 = 6 + c$, so $c = -3$. You now know that $g(x) = \frac{2}{3}x - 3$, so substitute $x = -6$ into this to get $g(-6) = \frac{2}{3}(-6) - 3$; $g(-6) = -4 - 3 = -7$. The answer is (A).

Compound Functions

Take a look at the following question:

5

If $f(x) = 6x - 3$ and $g(x) = 2x + 1$, what is $f(g(3))$?

A) 6

B) 24

C) 34

D) 39

This is called a compound function. Compound functions can look intimidating, but when you do them step-by-step, you apply the same concepts. Always start with the function on the inside. Solve for the value of $g(3)$: $g(3) = 2(3) + 1 = 7$. Now, replace $g(3)$ with 7 in the original question. The question now becomes what is $f(7)$? Plug 7 into $f(x)$ to get $f(7) = 6(7) - 3 = 39$.

Slope

Think back to this example in an earlier chapter:

> Kelly opens a bank account with an initial deposit, and then she makes a fixed deposit into the account once per week. The equation $B = 30x + 150$ models the amount of money in Kelly's bank account x weeks after she opens it.

This could be written in function notation as $f(x) = 30x + 150$, and in the xy-plane the graph would look like this.

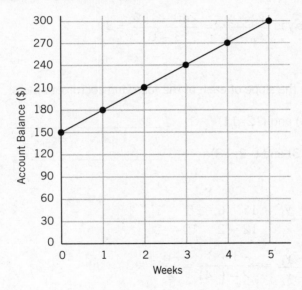

The output of a function is the y value, so this function could also be written $y = 30x + 150$. You may recognize this as *slope-intercept form*. An equation is in slope-intercept form when it is written in the format $y = mx + b$, where m and b are constants. When an equation is written in slope-intercept form, the m represents the slope, which is the amount that the y value increases per additional unit of x. In this case, it is the amount that Kelly deposits each week. The *b* represents the *y-intercept,* which is the value when $x = 0$. In this context, the *y*-intercept is Kelly's initial deposit.

Slope is calculated as $\dfrac{rise}{run}$ or $\dfrac{y_2 - y_1}{x_2 - x_1}$. To see this formula in action, you can pick any two coordinate pairs on the graph above. Try these two:

$(x_1, y_1) = (0, 150)$

$(x_2, y_2) = (3, 240)$

This gives you $\dfrac{y_2 - y_1}{x_2 - x_1} = \dfrac{240 - 150}{3 - 0} = 30$.

Calculate the slope of each of the following coordinate pairs:

1. (2, 6) and (12, 11)   _____

2. (−4, 3) and (−2, −3)   _____

Answers:

1. $\dfrac{y_2 - y_1}{x_2 - x_1} = \dfrac{11 - 6}{12 - 2} = \dfrac{5}{10} = \dfrac{1}{2}$.

2. $\dfrac{y_2 - y_1}{x_2 - x_1} = \dfrac{-3 - 3}{-2 - (-4)} = \dfrac{-6}{2} = -3$.

You can also calculate the *y*-intercept when given two coordinate pairs.

Consider the points (−4, 3) and (−2, −3) again. The slope was −3, so the equation in slope-intercept form is $y = -3x + b$. Now you can plug in either coordinate pair into this equation to solve for b: $y = -3x + b$ becomes $3 = -3(-4) + b$, which simplifies to $3 = 12 + b$, so $b = -9$. The equation of the line that passes through the points (−4, 3) and (−2, −3) is therefore $y = -3x - 9$.

Notice that the y-intercept and slope are both negative, so the graph looks like this:

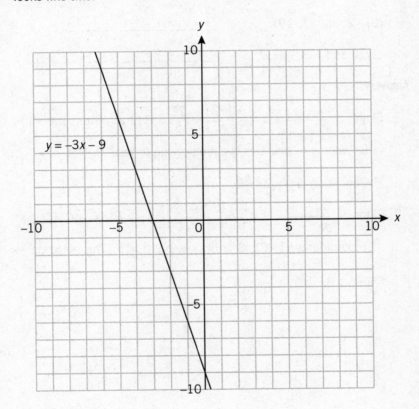

$y = -3x - 9$

> ## HINT
>
> Negative slopes mean the value decreases from left to right and positive slopes mean the value increases from left to right.

Write the equation in slope-intercept form for the line that passes through each of the following coordinate pairs:

1. $(0, -2)$ and $(7, 19)$ _____

2. $(1, 8)$ and $(-3, -4)$ _____

Answers:

1. Slope $= \dfrac{y_2 - y_1}{x_2 - x_1} = \dfrac{19 - (-2)}{7 - 0} = \dfrac{21}{7} = 3$; the y-intercept is the value when $x = 0$, so this is already given to you: $(0, -2)$; $b = -2$.

The equation is $y = 3x - 2$.

2. Slope $= \dfrac{y_2 - y_1}{x_2 - x_1} = \dfrac{-4 - 8}{-3 - 1} = \dfrac{-12}{-4} = 3$; $y = 3x + b$. Plug in the coordinates $(1, 8)$: $8 = 3(1) + b$; $b = 5$. The equation is

$y = 3x + 5$.

Parallel and Perpendicular Lines

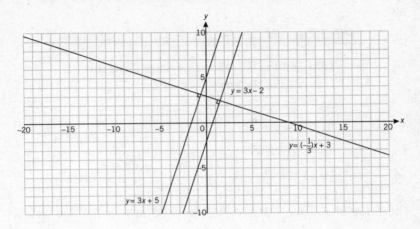

The two lines in the questions on the previous page are *parallel* because both have a slope of 3. Parallel lines are lines that have the same slope. *Perpendicular* lines are lines that intersect each other at a right angle. Perpendicular lines have slopes that are *negative reciprocals* of each other. A *negative reciprocal* is the value that results when the numerator and denominator are switched and the sign is changed. For example, the line $y = -\dfrac{1}{3}x + 3$ is perpendicular to both of these lines because $-\dfrac{1}{3}$ is the negative reciprocal of 3 (which can be written as the fraction $+\dfrac{3}{1}$).

Take a look at the following question:

6

Which of the following represents a line that is parallel to the line $y = 4x - 3$?

A) $4x + 3y = 2$

B) $4x + y = -3$

C) $8x - 2y = 7$

D) $x - 4y = 2$

The slope of $y = 4x - 3$ is 4, so you need to find the line with a slope of 4. In this case, the answer choices aren't in slope-intercept form, but rather in standard form: $Ax + By = C$. Try to rewrite (A) in slope-intercept form: $4x + 3y = 2$. Subtract $4x$ from each side to get $3y = -4x + 2$; then divide by 3 to get $y = -\frac{4}{3}x + \frac{2}{3}$. You can eliminate (A). Notice that the slope of $4x + 3y = 2$ is $-\frac{4}{3}$, which is $-\frac{A}{B}$. The slope of any line in standard form, $Ax + By = C$, is always $-\frac{A}{B}$. This means you can eliminate (B) as well because this slope will be negative, but the slope of the original line was positive. In (C), $A = 8$ and $B = -2$, so the slope is $-\frac{A}{B} = -\frac{8}{-2} = 4$. Choice (C) has a slope of 4, so it is parallel to the line $y = 4x - 3$.

Systems of Equations in the Coordinate Plane

Most problems related to systems of equations can be solved with the Stack and Add method, but there are a few additional things you need to know.

Consider the following system of equations:

$$3x + 4y = 16$$
$$9x + 12y = 24$$

If you wanted to solve this system with Stack and Add, you would multiply the first equation by -3 to get $-9x - 12y = -48$. Stack and Add then gives you the following result:

$$
\begin{array}{r}
-9x - 12y = -48 \\
+\ 9x + 12y = \ \ 24 \\
\hline
0 = -24
\end{array}
$$

The result $0 = -24$ is obviously not a true statement, so this system does not have a solution. This is because the two lines are parallel.

If you rewrote the equations in slope-intercept form, you would get $y = -\dfrac{3}{4}x + 4$ and $y = -\dfrac{3}{4}x + 2$, respectively. A system of parallel lines does not have a solution because parallel lines never intersect.

However, having the same slope does not necessarily mean the system has no solutions.

Consider the following system:

$$3x + 4y = 16$$
$$9x + 12y = 48$$

The slope of each of these is still $-\dfrac{3}{4}$. It's tempting to say there is no solution, but make sure that you look at the y-intercept as well. In slope-intercept form, both of these equations become $y = -\dfrac{3}{4}x + 4$. Both equations define the same line, so every point on this line is a solution. There are an infinite number of solutions to a system of equations if they represent the same line.

> ## HINT
> A system of parallel lines has no solution, a system that represents the same line has an infinite number of solutions, and all other systems of linear equations will have exactly one solution (at the intersection of the two lines).

Take a look at this question:

16

$$-ax + 5y = 9$$
$$7x - 4y = 11$$

If the system of equations above has no solution, what is the value of the constant a ?

If the system has no solutions, then the lines must be parallel. These are in standard form, so the slopes are $-\dfrac{A}{B} = \dfrac{a}{5}$ and $-\dfrac{A}{B} = -\dfrac{7}{-4} = \dfrac{7}{4}$.

Since the lines are parallel, you know that $\dfrac{a}{5} = \dfrac{7}{4}$. Cross-multiply to get $4a = 35$. Finally, divide by 4 to get $a = \dfrac{35}{4}$.

Your Turn—Exercise 8.1

5

If $f(x) = 3x + 1$, what is $f(-2x)$?

A) $x + 1$

B) $-6x + 1$

C) $-6x^2 + 1$

D) $-6x^2 - 2x$

15

x	$f(x)$
0	4
1	7
2	3
3	1

x	$g(x)$
1	1
2	3
3	2
4	0

The tables above show some values of the functions f and g. What is the value of $f(g(2))$?

A) 1

B) 3

C) 4

D) 7

8

Line m has a slope of 3 and passes through the point $(2, 9)$. Line n passes through the points $(2, 6)$ and $(3, 10)$. If the two lines intersect at (c, d), what is the value of $c - d$?

A) -13

B) -2

C) 3

D) 5

19

$$mx + ny = 8$$
$$3x + 5y = 48$$

If the system above has an infinite number of solutions, what is the value of $\dfrac{m}{n}$?

9

Line k has a y-intercept of -2 and contains the point (m, n). If $mn \neq 0$, what is the slope of line k in terms of m and n ?

A) $\dfrac{n + 2}{m}$

B) $\dfrac{m + 2}{n}$

C) $\dfrac{m - n}{-2}$

D) $\dfrac{n - 2}{m}$

22

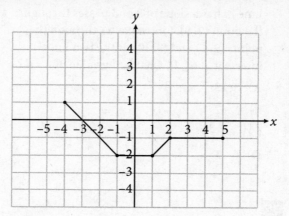

The graph of function f is shown above.
Which of the following is/are equal to -1?

    I. $f(-1)$

    II. $f(2)$

    III. $f\left(\dfrac{5}{2}\right)$

A) I only

B) II only

C) II and III only

D) I, II, and III

27

A line with a negative slope and a positive *y*-intercept does NOT pass through which of the following quadrants?

A) Quadrant I

B) Quadrant II

C) Quadrant III

D) Quadrant IV

Answers and Explanations to Exercise 8.1

5. **B** In this question, the input of the function is $-2x$ instead of x, so this is what you replace x with in the function:

$f(-2x) = 3(-2x) + 1 = -6x + 1$, which is (B).

You could also have used Plugging In to help you understand this question. Set $x = 2$. Therefore, you can rewrite the question "what is the value of $f(-4)$?" The input for the function is -4: $f(-4) = 3(-4) + 1 = -12 + 1 = -11$. If you check all of the answers with $x = 2$, you will see that only (B) gives you -11.

15. **A** Start with the function on the inside. According to the second table, the value of $g(2)$ is 3, so the question is asking for $f(3)$. Use the first table to find $f(3) = 1$.

8. **A** Write the equations for each of these lines. Line m has a slope of 3, so the equation is $y = 3x + b$. Plug in the point $(2, 9)$ to solve for b: $9 = 3(2) + b$, so $b = 3$. The equation for line m is $y = 3x + 3$. Now, solve for the slope of line n: $\dfrac{y_2 - y_1}{x_2 - x_1} = \dfrac{10 - 6}{3 - 2} = 4$. Plug in the point $(2, 6)$ into $y = 4x + b$ to get $6 = 4(2) + b$; $b = -2$. The equation for line n is $y = 4x - 2$. At the intersection the y values are the same, so you can set these two equations equal to each other to get $3x + 3 = 4x - 2$. Subtract 3 from both sides to get $3x = 4x - 5$, then subtract $4x$ from both sides to get

$-x = -5$, so $x = 5$. Be careful though, the question asked for $x - y$. You can solve for y by putting $x = 5$ in either equation: $y = 3(5) + 3 = 18$. The value of $x - y = 5 - 18 = -13$.

19. $\dfrac{3}{5}$ If there are an infinite number of solutions, then the two lines are the same. If you rearranged the equations into slope-intercept form, you would get $y = \dfrac{-m}{n}x + \dfrac{8}{n}$ and $y = -\dfrac{3}{5}x + \dfrac{48}{5}$. You can ignore the constants in this case and focus on the fact that the lines must have the same slope, so $\dfrac{-m}{n} = -\dfrac{3}{5}$, and $\dfrac{m}{n} = \dfrac{3}{5}$.

Note that this does not mean that $m = 3$ and $n = 5$. It only gives you the relationship between the two, which is all you needed for this question. If you truly needed to solve for the values of m and n individually, then you need to set the constant term in both equations to the same value, 48. To do this you can multiply the first equation by 6 to get $6mx + 6ny = 48$. Now, you can see that if $6mx + 6ny = 48$ is the same line as

$3x + 5y = 48$, then $6m = 3$ and $6n = 5$. Therefore, $m = \dfrac{1}{2}$ and $n = \dfrac{5}{6}$. The value of $\dfrac{m}{n} = \dfrac{\frac{1}{2}}{\frac{5}{6}} = \dfrac{1}{2} \times \dfrac{6}{5} = \dfrac{6}{10} = \dfrac{3}{5}$. You should do all of these steps only if the question requires

you to solve for the actual values of the terms rather than

the quotient.

9. **A** If the y-intercept is -2, then the point $(0, -2)$ is on the line. You can plug in any values for m and n (except 0 since $mn \neq 0$). Say $m = 4$ and $n = 3$. You have two coordinate pairs, $(0, -2)$ and $(4, 3)$, so the slope is $\dfrac{y_2 - y_1}{x_2 - x_1} = \dfrac{3 - (-2)}{4 - 0} = \dfrac{5}{4}$. If you plug $m = 4$ and $n = 3$ into the answers, only (A) gives you $\dfrac{5}{4}$.

22. **C** Use POE. Start with statement I: $f(-1)$ is the y value when $x = -1$. The function passes through $(-1, -2)$, so $f(-1) = -2$. Eliminate (A) and (D). Since II is in both of the remaining answer choices, check statement III. When $x = \dfrac{5}{2}$, $y = -1$, so statement III is true. The answer is (C).

27. **C** Sketch this graph. A positive *y*-intercept means that at *x* = 0, *y* > 0, and a negative slope means the line decreases from left to right. Your graph should look something like this:

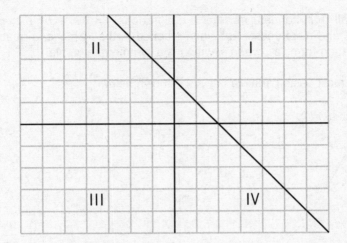

The quadrants are labeled in the graph above as well. No matter how you draw the graph, as long as the *y*-intercept is positive and the slope is negative, it will always pass through quadrants I, II, and IV.

Nonlinear Functions

Parabolas

Recall that standard form for a quadratic is $y = ax^2 + bx + c$, where a, b, and c are constants. When graphed in the xy-plane, a quadratic equation forms a *parabola*, which is a symmetrical curve.

The most basic parabola is $y = x^2$, shown below.

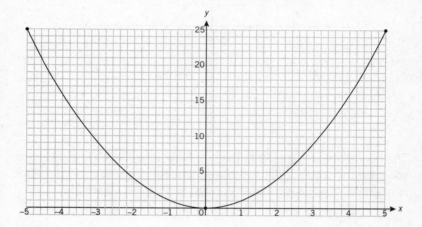

Consider the standard form equation for the parabola $y = x^2 + 4x - 12$. Can you describe what this graph looks like? Where are its zeros? What is its vertex? Likely you cannot answer any of these questions without doing some rearranging. The standard form equation for a parabola is not very useful if you want to identify key features of the graph. Instead, you will want the equation in intercept or vertex form.

Intercept Form

Intercept form is useful for determining the zeros of a function. Converting a standard form parabola to intercept form is exactly the same process as factoring a quadratic: find the binomial factors.

$$y = x^2 + 4x - 12$$
$$y = (x + 6)(x - 2)$$

Recall that you need two constants that add to 4 and multiply to -12. To verify that these are the correct factors, use FOIL on $(x + 6)(x - 2)$. You get $y = x^2 - 2x + 6x - 12$, which is equal to the original equation.

Therefore, the zeros of this equation are the values where each of these factors is equal to zero: $(x + 6) = 0$; $x = -6$ and $(x - 2) = 0$; $x = 2$.

6

$$y = x^2 + 2x - 15$$

Which of the following equivalent forms of the equation above displays the x-intercepts of the parabola as constants?

A) $y = x(x + 2) - 15$

B) $y = (x + 5)(x - 3)$

C) $y = (x + 1)^2 - 16$

D) $y + 15 = x^2 + 2x$

The nice thing about a question like this is that it doesn't even require you to put the equation in intercept form yourself, only to recognize which form you need. Since an x-intercept is the same thing as the zero of a function, the answer is (B).

> ## HINT
>
> If the question requires you to identify the x-intercepts or zeros of a function, then you want the equation in intercept form.

Vertex Form

Some questions will require you to find the vertex, or the point where the parabola crosses its axis of symmetry. To do this, you will need to write the equation in *vertex form*.

The vertex form for a parabola is $y = a(x - h) + k$, where a is a constant and (h, k) is the vertex.

The vertex is the minimum value for a parabola where $a > 0$ (a parabola that opens upward) and the maximum value for a parabola where $a < 0$ (a parabola that opens downward).

Take a look at the following question:

10

Which of the following is an equivalent form of the parabola $y = x^2 - 4x + 3$ that identifies the coordinates of the parabola as constants in the equation?

A) $y = (x - 2)^2 - 1$

B) $y = (x - 3)(x - 1)$

C) $y = x(x - 4) + 3$

D) $y = (x + 1)(x - 3)$

Similar to the previous question, this question only requires you to recognize that you need vertex form to identify the vertex. Only (A) is in vertex form, $y = a(x - h) + k$. The vertex of this equation is $(h, k) = (2, -1)$.

> ## HINT
>
> If the question asks for the vertex or the minimum or maximum value of a parabola, you need the equation in vertex form: $y = a(x - h) + k$.

Try another:

26

$$y = (x + 1)(x - 7)$$

Which of the following is the equivalent form of the function above that identifies the minimum value as a constant or coefficient in the equation?

A) $y = x^2 - 6x - 7$

B) $y = (x - 3)^2 - 7$

C) $y = x^2 - 16$

D) $y = (x - 3)^2 - 16$

The question is asking for the minimum value, which is at the vertex, so you need vertex form. You can eliminate (A) because this is standard form. However, the remaining choices are in vertex form, so for this question you actually need to know how to write a quadratic equation in vertex form.

$$y = (x + 1)(x - 7)$$

First you need to get this from intercept form to standard form. You can do this with FOIL: $y = x^2 - 7x + x - 7$, which simplifies to $y = x^2 - 6x - 7$.

Next, you need to *complete the square*:

$$y = x^2 - 6x - 7$$

Move the constant term to the left side of the equation by adding 7 to both sides:

$$y + 7 = x^2 - 6x$$

Now, you want the expression on the right in the form of a perfect square. Remember that $(x + a)^2 = x^2 + 2ax + a^2$. Therefore, to find the a in the perfect square $(x + a)^2$, divide the coefficient on x by 2. In this case the coefficient is −6, so $a = -3$, and the perfect square that you want is $(x - 3)^2 = x^2 - 6x + 9$. You need to add 9 to each side of the equation to form this perfect square on the right:

$$y + 7 + 9 = x^2 - 6x + 9$$

$$y + 16 = (x - 3)^2$$

Finally, subtract the constant term from both sides.

$$y = (x - 3)^2 - 16$$

The answer is (D). The vertex of this equation is (3, −16), and the minimum value is −16. The graph on the next page is the graph of this equation.

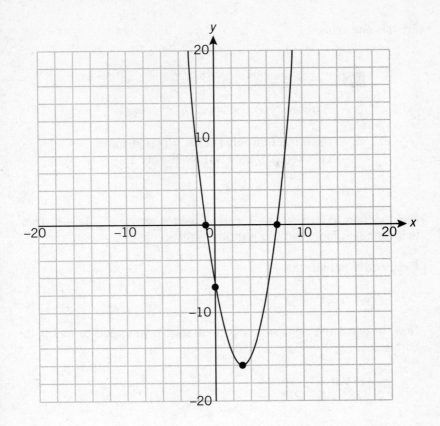

Try this one yourself:

16

$$f(x) = x^2 - 4x - 5$$

If the minimum value of the function above occurs at (c, d), what is the value of c ?

The function $f(x) = x^2 - 4x - 5$ can be written as $y = x^2 - 4x - 5$. This is in standard form, but you want the equation in vertex form.

First, add 5 to both sides:

$$y + 5 = x^2 - 4x$$

Now, to make the right side a perfect square you need to add 4 to both sides:

$$y + 9 = x^2 - 4x + 4$$
$$y + 9 = (x - 2)^2$$

Finally, subtract the 9 from both sides to get:

$$y = (x - 2)^2 - 9$$

The vertex of this equation is $(2, -9)$, so this means that the minimum value, $y = -9$, occurs at $x = 2$. Therefore, $c = 2$.

Circles

Although circles are not functions, they fit here nicely because completing the square is also useful when working with the equation of a circle.

The standard form, also called center-radius form, for the equation of a circle is as follows:

$(x - h)^2 + (y - k)^2 = r^2$, where (h, k) is the center of the circle and r is the radius.

For example, the equation $(x - 2)^2 + (y + 3)^2 = 9$ defines a circle with a center at $(2, -3)$ and a radius of 3.

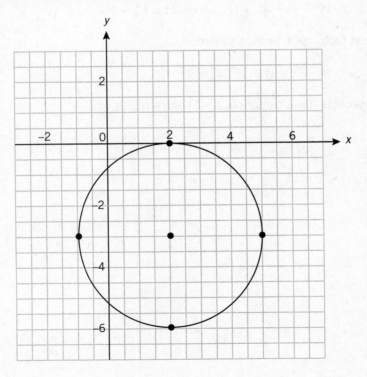

However, sometimes an equation is given in general form instead:

$$x^2 + y^2 + 2x - 4x = 11$$

In these cases you need to complete the square to identify the radius and center.

To complete the square for a circle, move the x terms together and the y terms together:

$$(x^2 - 4x) + (y^2 + 2x) = 11$$

You need to make each of these a perfect square:

$$(x^2 - 4x + 4) + (y^2 + 2x + 1) = 11 + 4 + 1$$

Then factor each perfect square:

$$(x - 2)^2 + (y + 1)^2 = 16$$

This circle has a center of $(2, -1)$ and a radius of 4.

Take a look at this question:

25

Which of the following is the equation of a circle in the xy-plane with a center of $(2, 0)$ if the point $\left(4, \dfrac{3}{2}\right)$ is on the circle?

A) $(x + 2)^2 + y^2 = \dfrac{5}{2}$

B) $(x - 2)^2 + y^2 = \dfrac{25}{4}$

C) $(x + 2)^2 + y^2 = \dfrac{25}{4}$

D) $(x - 2)^2 + y^2 = \dfrac{5}{2}$

There are a couple of ways to tackle this question. Start with the most straightforward piece of information. If the center of the circle is at $(2, 0)$, then the left side of the equation needs to be $(x - 2)^2 + y^2$, so eliminate (A) and (C). The easiest thing to do at this point is actually to plug the point $\left(4, \dfrac{3}{2}\right)$ into one of the two remaining equations. If the point is on the circle, the equation will be true when you plug in the point. Try (B): $(4 - 2)^2 + \left(\dfrac{3}{2}\right)^2 = \dfrac{25}{4}$. This becomes $4 + \dfrac{9}{4} = \dfrac{25}{4}$, which is $\dfrac{16}{4} + \dfrac{9}{4} = \dfrac{25}{4}$. This statement is true, so the answer is (B).

Identifying Graphs

Sometimes you will be asked to identify the graph that matches an equation or the equation that matches a graph. For linear equations you should use the concepts of intercepts and slope, and for quadratics you should use the vertex and *x*-intercepts (zeros). You can apply the ideas of intercepts to other polynomials as well.

Take a look at this question:

16

The graph of a function $g(x)$ has x-intercepts at –2, 1, and 4. Which of the following could be the function g?

A) $g(x) = (x + 2)(x + 1)(x - 4)$

B) $g(x) = (x + 2)(x - 1) + 4$

C) $g(x) = (x + 2)(x - 1)(x - 4)$

D) $g(x) = (x - 2)^2(x + 1)$

If the function has an *x*-intercept at $x = -2$, this means that this is a zero of the function and $(x + 2)$ must therefore be a factor. You can eliminate (D) because it does not include $(x + 2)$ as a factor. Similarly, an intercept at $x = 1$ means that $(x - 1)$ is a factor, so you can eliminate (A). Lastly, $(x - 4)$ must be a factor. The answer is (C).

For more free content, visit <u>PrincetonReview.com</u>

This graph would look like this:

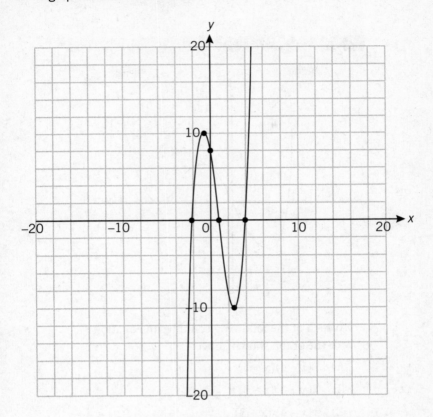

However, some polynomial graphs are a little more complicated.

Take a look at this one:

 12

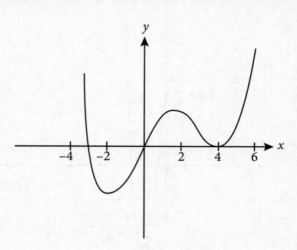

Which of the following could be an equation for the graph shown above?

A) $x(x - 4)(x + 3)$

B) $x(x + 4)(x - 3)$

C) $x(x - 4)^2(x + 3)$

D) $x(x + 4)^2(x - 3)$

In this case it isn't enough to know the intercepts. Using the intercepts, you can figure out that $x = -3$ means that $(x + 3)$ is a factor, so eliminate (B) and (D). You also know that since $x = 0$ and $x = 4$ are x-intercepts, then x and $(x - 4)$ must be factors, but these are both in (A) and (C). To choose between (A) and (C), you need to use the degree of the function.

The degree of a function is the largest exponent on x when the function is written in standard form. For instance, $y = x^3 + 3x^2 + 7x$ has a degree of 3. The function $y = x^2(x + 3)$ also has a degree of 3 because if you expanded it out, you would get $y = x^3 + 3x^2$. A function of degree 3 can have at most two turning points. The graph of $y = x^3 + 3x^2$ is shown below.

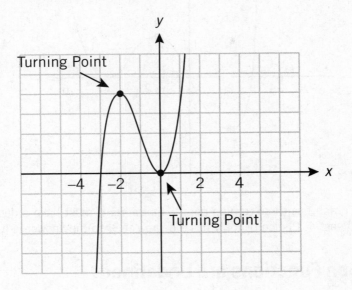

A turning point is a point where the function changes direction. At $x = -2$ the function changes from increasing to decreasing, and at $x = 0$ the function changes from decreasing to increasing.

A function with n turning points must have a degree of at least $n + 1$.

Look back at the function in the question.

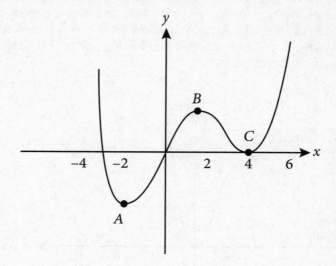

This graph has three turning points; therefore, it must have a degree of at least 4. Choice (A) only has a degree of 3, so the answer is (C).

When Functions are Undefined

You may be asked for the values of x for which a function is undefined. These are values that will cause you to have a denominator of zero or to take a root of a negative number. You may have learned the term domain in math class as the values of x that do work in a function, but the SAT does not use that term. Instead, you may see a question like the one below.

Try this one:

34

$$f(x) = \frac{1}{(x-2)^2 - 6(x-3) + 3}$$

If a is a constant and the function f above is undefined for $x = a$, what is the value of a ?

When a function is a rational expression, the function is undefined whenever the denominator is zero. So, the question can be rewritten as follows: For what value of x does $(x-2)^2 - 6(x-3) + 3 = 0$?

Expand this out to $x^2 - 4x + 4 - 6x + 18 + 3$, then collect like terms to get $x^2 - 10x + 25$. This is a perfect square, so it factors to $0 = (x-5)^2$. The function is undefined when $x = 5$, so $a = 5$.

Linear and Exponential Growth

Take a look at the following question:

8

The membership of a club increases by 20% per year since its inception. Which type of relationship exists between the membership of the club and time since the club was formed?

A) An increasing linear relationship

B) A quadratic relationship in which more members corresponds to a longer time since inception

C) A decreasing linear relationship

D) An exponential relationship in which fewer members corresponds to a shorter time since inception

To answer this question you need to know the difference between *linear growth* and *exponential growth*. With linear growth, a value increases by the same amount per year. Think of Kelly's bank account again: $y = 30x + 150$. This is linear growth because each week her account increases by the same amount, $30. However, consider the club in the question above. If there are 100 members at inception, then the club increases by 20 members the first year. The second year the club would increase by 20% of 120, which is 24. This is exponential growth, rather than linear growth. With exponential growth or decay, the rate of change in the function is dependent on the current value. Larger values increase, or decrease, more rapidly. The two graphs below demonstrate exponential growth and decay. The graph on the top shows the membership of the club with 100 members that grows at a rate of 20% per year, while the graph on the bottom demonstrates the membership of a club with 100 members that decreases at a rate of 20% per year.

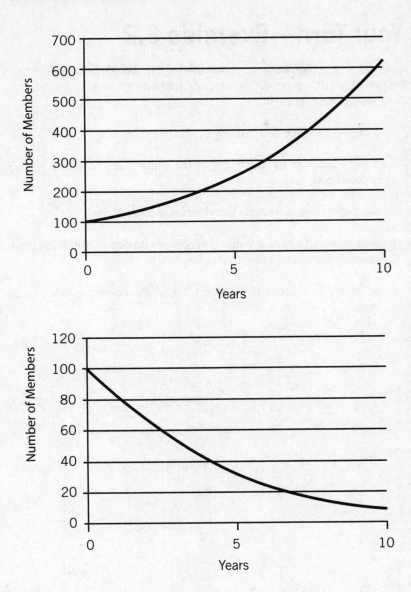

Your Turn—Exercise 8.2

Determine whether each of the following situations describes exponential growth, exponential decay, increasing linear growth, or decreasing linear growth:

1. a car whose value decreases by $2,000 per year.

2. a bank account in which 3% of the initial value is added to the account each year.

3. the population of bacteria that doubles each day.

4. the balance of a bank account that receives no deposits and charges a monthly fee of $10 a month.

5. an investment account that loses 3% of the current balance each year.

Answers and Explanations to Exercise 8.2

1. The rate is negative and constant: decreasing linear.

2. Even though it says 3%, it's always 3% of the same value; therefore the rate is positive and constant: increasing linear.

3. Each day the population is twice the previous day's population. If the population starts at 1, then it will increase by 1 the first day, but then double from 2 to 4 on the second day. The rate increases as the population increases: exponential growth.

4. The bank account decreases by $10 per month: decreasing linear.

5. The investment account decreases by 3% of the current value each year, so as the value decreases, the rate of decrease decreases: exponential decay.

You may be required to write the equation for a situation with exponential growth or decay. The basic formula is $y = A(1 \pm r)^t$, where A represents the initial value, r is the rate of increase (or decrease if $r < 0$), and t is the number of time intervals that have passed. For example, a bank account with an initial balance of 100 that earns 5% interest each year would have a balance of $y = 100(1 + 0.05)^t$ after t years.

27

A company's research and development budget decreases by 15% every 5 years. If the current budget is $75,000, what will the budget be n years from now?

A) $75{,}000(0.15)^n$

B) $75{,}000(0.85)^{5n}$

C) $75{,}000(0.85)^{\frac{n}{5}}$

D) $75{,}000(0.15)^{5n}$

Use the formula $y = A(1 \pm r)^t$. The initial value, A, is 75,000. The budget decreases by 15% each year, so $r = -0.15$, and the t is $\frac{n}{5}$ because it changes only every 5 years instead of every year. This gives you $y = A(1 \pm r)^t = 75{,}000(1 - 0.15)^{\frac{n}{5}}$, which matches (C). If you got stuck between (B) and (C), you can always pick a value and test the function. Say that $n = 5$. Then the function should decrease by 15% once. This matches (C). Choice (B) means that the function decreases by 15% five times a year.

Consider again the scenario in which the population of bacteria doubles every day. You can use the same formula as above. In this case, the rate of increase is 100% because each day you add the whole value of the population again. This becomes $y = A(1 + 1)^t = A(2)^t$, where A is the initial population and t is the time. If the population tripled each day, then you would add 2 times the value of the population each day, and the equation would be $y = A(1 + 2)^t = A(3)^t$.

Your Turn—Exercise 8.3

4

What is the vertex of the parabola defined by the equation $y = x^2 + 4x - 12$?

A) $(0, -12)$

B) $(-6, 0)$

C) $(-2, -16)$

D) $(2, -12)$

8

What is the standard form of the equation of the circle defined by the equation $x^2 + y^2 - 6x + 8y = 0$?

A) $(x - 6)^2 + (y + 8)^2 = 0$

B) $(x + 3)^2 + (y + 4)^2 = 25$

C) $(x - 3)^2 + (y + 4)^2 = 25$

D) $(x - 3)^2 + (y + 4)^2 = 5$

11

The function $f(x)$ has $(x + 2)$ as one of its factors. Which of the following must be true about the graph of $f(x)$?

A) $f(x)$ includes the point $(2, 0)$

B) $f(x)$ includes the point $(0, 2)$

C) $f(x)$ includes the point $(-2, 0)$

D) $f(x)$ includes the point $(0, -2)$

31

Sean and David both open savings accounts at the same time with an initial deposit of $150. Sean earns 4% interest annually on his account and David earns 3% interest annually on his account. If neither makes any additional deposits, after 10 years how much greater, in dollars, is Sean's account balance than David's account balance? Round your answer to the nearest dollar.

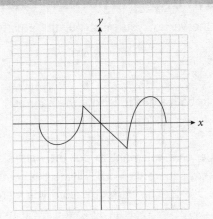

The graph of $y = f(x)$ is shown above. Which of the following represents the graph of $y = |f(x)|$?

A)
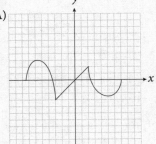

B)
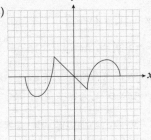

C)
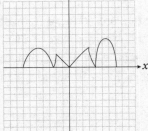

D)
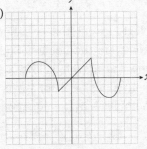

Answers and Explanations to Exercise 8.3

4. **C** To find the vertex, you must put the equation into vertex form:

$$y = x^2 + 4x - 12$$

Add 12 to both sides to isolate the x terms:

$$y + 12 = x^2 + 4x$$

Remember that you want to put the right side in the form of a perfect square: $(x + a)^2$. Divide the coefficient on x by 2 to get $a = 2$. The perfect square you want on the right side is $(x + 2)^2 = x^2 + 4x + 4$. You need to add 4 to both sides of this equation:

$$y + 12 + 4 = x^2 + 4x + 4$$

Now factor:

$$y + 16 = (x + 2)^2$$

Finally, subtract 16 to get $y = (x + 2)^2 - 16$.

In vertex form: $y = (x - h)^2 + k$ the vertex is (h, k), so the vertex of $y = (x + 2)^2 - 16$ is $(-2, -16)$, (C).

8. **C** Start by rewriting the equation with the x terms and y terms listed together:

$$x^2 - 6x + y^2 + 8y = 0$$

Next, to get the equation into standard form, you must complete the square. Start with the x terms. Take half of the coefficient on the x (-6), square it, and add that to both sides. Half of -6 is -3, and $(-3)^2$ is 9, so add 9 to both sides of the equation:

$$x^2 - 6x + 9 + y^2 + 8y = 9$$

Now $x^2 - 6x + 9$ is a perfect square; it factors into $(x - 3)^2$, so you can rewrite the equation:

$$(x - 3)^2 + y^2 + 8y = 9$$

You can do the same to the y terms. Half of 8 is 4, and $4^2 = 16$, so add 16 to both sides of the equation:

$$(x - 3)^2 + y^2 + 8y + 16 = 9 + 16$$

Now $y^2 + 8y + 16$ is a perfect square; it factors into $(x + 4)^2$, so you can rewrite the equation again:

$$(x - 3)^2 + (y + 4)^2 = 25$$

That matches (C). Note you do not need to take the square root of 25; that would change the value of the equation. Instead, the radius is left squared.

11. **C** If $(x + 2)$ is one of the factors of $f(x)$, then $f(x) = 0$ when $(x + 2) = 0$. Solving $(x + 2) = 0$ for x shows you that $x = -2$. This means that, on the graph of $f(x)$, when $x = -2$, $y = 0$. Point $(-2, 0)$ therefore must be included in the graph of $f(x)$; this is (C).

31. **20** Both accounts experience exponential growth. Sean's account balance can be represented by the equation $y = 150(1.04)^t$, which after 10 years has a value of $150(1.04)^{10} \approx \$222.04$. David's account balance can be represented by the equation $y = 150(1.03)^t$, which has a value of approximately \$201.59 when $t = 10$. The difference between the accounts is (approximately) \$222.04 − \$201.59 = 20.45. The question says to round to the nearest dollar, so round to 20.

22. **C** It can be helpful to think of this question in terms of possible *y* values. Since the question asked for the graph of $y = |f(x)|$ and absolute value can never be negative, this function will have a graph with only positive values of *y*. Only (C) has a graph will all value for $y \geq 0$.

Step 9: Additional Math Topics

The SAT refers to all geometry questions as "Additional Topics." There are at most 6 of these questions on the test, so they won't play a big part in determining your score. Only cover this chapter after you are confident with the material in the previous chapters. Both sections of the Math test will begin with the following reference box, in case you forget a formula, and this chapter will cover the most important geometry concepts.

Reference Information

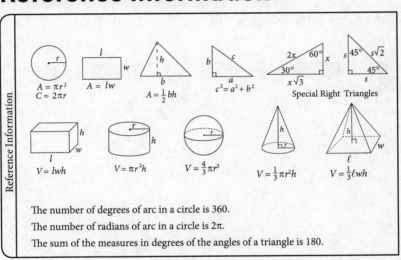

The number of degrees of arc in a circle is 360.

The number of radians of arc in a circle is 2π.

The sum of the measures in degrees of the angles of a triangle is 180.

Circles

The basic formulas for circles are as follows:

$$A = \pi r^2$$
$$C = 2\pi r$$

A circle with a radius of 5 has a diameter of 10, a circumference of 10π, and an area of 25π.

Take a look at the following:

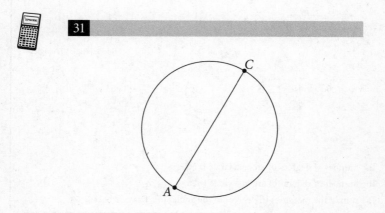

31

If *AC* is the diameter of the circle shown above, and the length of the arc *AC* is 6π, what is the radius of the circle?

If the arc of half of the circle has a length of 6π, then the circumference must be 12π. Circumference = $2\pi r = 12\pi$; $r = 6$.

Now consider this one:

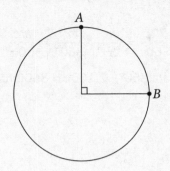

If the length of minor arc AB is 2π, what is the
radius of the circle?

The term *minor arc* just means the length of the shortest arc
between points A and B, clockwise around the circle, instead of the
counterclockwise.

A right angle is $\dfrac{1}{4}$ of a circle, so you can set up a proportion: $\dfrac{1}{4} = \dfrac{2\pi}{circumference}$. Cross-multiply to find that the circumference is 8π,

so $8\pi = 2\pi r$; the radius is 4.

You knew that a right angle was $\dfrac{1}{4}$ of a circle because $\dfrac{90°}{360°} = \dfrac{1}{4}$.

You can use this idea to solve any arc length problem.

$$\frac{central\ angle}{360°} = \frac{arc}{circumference}$$

The left side solves for the portion of the circle that is included in the central angle, so the arc must be the same portion of the circumference. Say you were asked to find the arc length for a sector with an angle measure of 72° and a radius of 15. The proportion would look like this:

$$\frac{72°}{360°} = \frac{arc}{2\pi r} \; ; \; \frac{72°}{360°} = \frac{arc}{30\pi}$$

$$72°(30\pi) = arc(360°); \; 2{,}160\pi = 360(arc); \; arc = 6\pi$$

Take a look at this question:

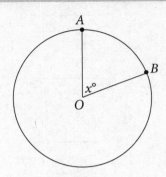

24

If $75 \leq x \leq 85$, and the radius of the circle above is 6, which of the following is a possible value for the length of minor arc AB?

A) 2.5

B) 7.5

C) 8

D) 9

Set up the proportion with 75° as the central angle. $\dfrac{75°}{360°} = \dfrac{AB}{2\pi(6)}$; $\dfrac{75°}{360°} = \dfrac{AB}{12\pi}$. Cross-multiply to get $75(12\pi) = AB(360)$. Divide by 360 to get $AB = 2.5\pi$. Be careful though; the answer choices are not in terms of π. Since $2.5\pi \approx 7.85$, and 75° is the lowest possible value for x, the arc length must be greater than or equal to 7.85. Eliminate (A) and (B). The answer is (C). Choice (D) must be too big because there can be only one answer within the possible range.

Practice working with circles with the following problems:

Radius = _____

Diameter = _____

Circumference = 16π

Area = _____

Radius = _____

Diameter = _____

Circumference = _____

Area = 9π

1.

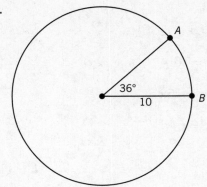

Length of arc $AB =$ _____

2.

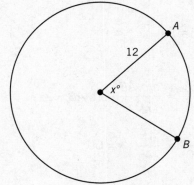

arc $AB = 4\pi$ $x =$ _____

Answers and Explanations:

Radius = $r = 8$

Diameter = $2r = 16$

Circumference = $2\pi r = 16\pi$

Area = $\pi r^2 = 64\pi$

Radius = $r = 3$

Diameter = $2r = 6$

Circumference = $2\pi r = 6\pi$

Area = $\pi r^2 = 9\pi$

1. $\dfrac{36°}{360°} = \dfrac{arc\ AB}{2\pi(10)}$; $\dfrac{36°}{360°} = \dfrac{arc\ AB}{20\pi}$; arc $AB = 2\pi$

2. $\dfrac{x°}{360°} = \dfrac{4\pi}{2\pi(12)}$; $\dfrac{x°}{360°} = \dfrac{4\pi}{24\pi}$; $x = 60°$

Angles

Parallel Lines

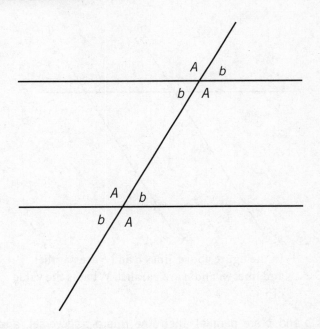

When a pair of parallel lines is cut by a transversal, as shown above, all of the angles marked *A* are equal to each other and all of the angles marked *b* are equal to each other. *A* and *b* are supplementary angles. Supplementary angles add to 180°.

Take a look at this one:

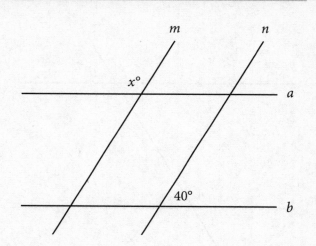

32

In the figure above, lines *a* and *b* are parallel
and lines *m* and *n* are parallel. What is the value
of *x*?

If lines *a* and *b* are parallel, then line *n* is a transversal, and all of
the acute angles formed by this transversal are 40°. Consequently,
all of the obtuse angles are the supplementary angle to 40°,
180° − 40° = 140°.

You are also told that *m* and *n* are parallel, which means that line *a* is
a transversal to this pair of parallel lines, and all of these acute angles
are also 40°, and all of the obtuse angles are 140°. The value of *x* is
140°.

Whenever two pairs of parallel lines intersect, all resulting acute
angles are equivalent, and all obtuse angles are equivalent.

Vertical Angles

Take a look at this question:

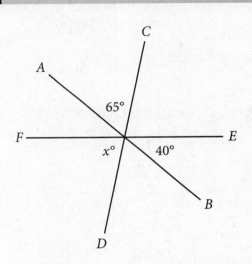

16

Note: Figure not drawn to scale.

In the figure above, lines *AB, CD,* and *EF*
intersect at a point. What is the value of *x* ?

Take this one step at a time. All lines have a total of 180°, so you can
solve for the angle between 65° and 40° with $180 - 65 - 40 = 75°$.

This angle and the angle marked *x*° are *vertical angles.* Vertical angles
are the angles directly opposite each other at the intersection of two
lines. This means that $x = 75$.

Triangles

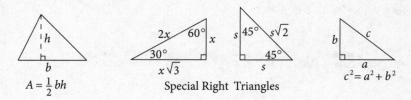

$A = \frac{1}{2}bh$

Special Right Triangles

$c^2 = a^2 + b^2$

Take a look at this triangle:

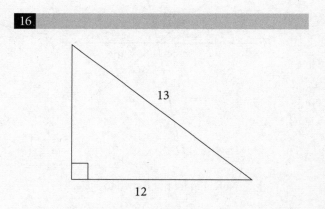

16

13

12

Note: Figure not drawn to scale.

What is the area of triangle *ABC*, shown above?

The area of a triangle is given by the formula $A = \frac{1}{2}bh$. The base of this triangle is 12, but the height isn't given. In order to find the height, you need to use the Pythagorean theorem: $a^2 + b^2 = c^2$, where *a* and *b* represent the legs of the right triangle and *c* is the hypotenuse. In this case the Pythagorean theorem gives you $12^2 + b^2 = 13^2$, which simplifies to $144 + b^2 = 169$; $b^2 = 25$; $b = 5$. Now that you know both the height of the triangle, 5, and the base of the triangle, 12, you can solve for the area: $A = \dfrac{1}{2}(12)(5) = 30$. You may have noticed that this triangle is a Pythagorean triple. Be on the lookout for those, as knowing the relationships of the sides on the triples can save you time.

The Pythagorean theorem can also be used to solve for distance.

Take a look at this question:

4

What is the distance between (3, 1) and (8, 4) ?

A) $\sqrt{28}$

B) $\sqrt{34}$

C) 7

D) 8

If you sketch this, you can form a triangle.

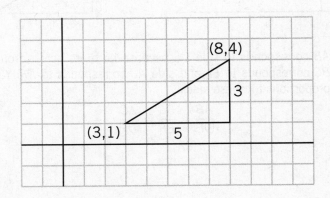

The base of the triangle is the horizontal distance ($8 - 3 = 5$), and the height of the triangle is the vertical distance ($4 - 1 = 3$). The distance between these two points is the hypotenuse of this triangle, so you can use the Pythagorean theorem to solve for it.

$$5^2 + 3^2 = c^2; \quad 34 = c^2$$

The distance is $\sqrt{34}$, (B).

Similar Triangles

Two triangles are similar if they have the same angle measures. With similar triangles the ratio of corresponding sides is constant, so you can use proportions to solve for missing side lengths. For example, the two triangles below are similar because both have angles of 90° and 35°, and therefore the unmarked angle in both of them is $180 - 90 - 35 = 55°$.

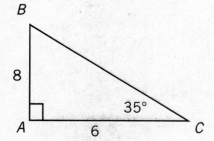 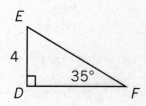

Side *AB* corresponds to side *DE* because both are across from 35°. Side *BC* corresponds to *EF* and side *AC* corresponds to *DF*. You can write proportions for these sides:

$$\frac{AB}{DE} = \frac{BC}{EF} = \frac{AC}{DF}.$$

For more free content, visit PrincetonReview.com

You could solve for side *DF* with this proportion: $\dfrac{8}{4} = \dfrac{6}{DF}$. Cross-multiply to get $24 = 8(DF)$, so $DF = 3$.

Take a look at the following question:

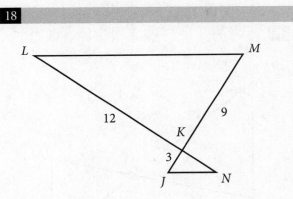

In the figure above, $\overline{JN} \parallel \overline{LM}$ and segment *JM* intersects segment *LN* at *K*. What is the length of segment *LN* ?

Here you have a pair of parallel lines. In this case, both *LN* and *JM* can be considered transversals. This means that angle *L* = angle *N* and angle *M* = angle *J*. Use this information to help you determine which sides of these similar triangles correspond to one another. The correct proportions are as follows:

$$\frac{JK}{KM} = \frac{KN}{KL}$$

Now solve for *KN*:

$$\frac{3}{9} = \frac{KN}{12}$$

Cross-multiply to get $36 = 9(KN)$, so $KN = 4$.

But be careful! The problem asked you to find the length of *LN*, not *KN*. Since *LK* is 12, add 12 and 4 to get *LN* = 16.

Sometimes similar triangles are used in real-world examples. Take a look at the following question:

17

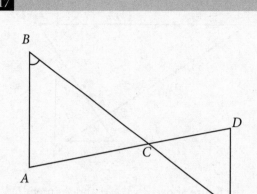

The map above shows 5 towns, *A*, *B*, *C*, *D*, and *E*. The distances represented by *CD*, *DE*, *CE*, and *AC* are 5 miles, 8 miles, 6 miles, and 30 miles, respectively. How far, in miles, is town *A* from town *B* ?

There is a lot of information in this question, so start by labeling the values you are given in the diagram. You also know that the vertical angles on either side of *C* are congruent, so you can mark this. Lastly, since both triangles have two congruent angles, the remaining angles must be congruent as well.

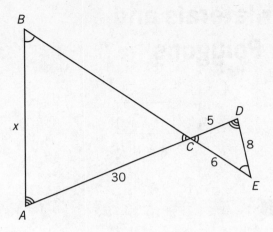

You have two similar triangles, so you can set up a proportion. *AC* and *CD* are corresponding sides (because both are across from congruent angles), and *AB* and *DE* are corresponding sides. You can set up the proportion $\dfrac{AC}{CD} = \dfrac{AB}{DE}$; $\dfrac{30}{5} = \dfrac{x}{8}$. Cross-multiply to get $5x = 240$, so $x = 48$.

Quadrilaterals and Other Polygons

$$A = lw$$

31

The length of a rectangle is 4 inches more than the width. If the area of the rectangle is 96, what is the length of the rectangle?

Whenever you are given a geometry question without a figure, the first thing you should do is draw it. If the length is 4 more than the width, you can call the width w and the length $(w + 4)$.

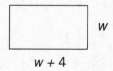

The area of a rectangle is $A = lw$, so $96 = w(w + 4)$. Distribute the right side of this equation to get $96 = w^2 + 4w$. Now, subtract 96 from both sides to get $0 = w^2 + 4w - 96$. This factors to $0 = (w + 12)(w - 8)$, and the roots are $w = 8$ and $w = -12$. Since the width can't be negative, w must be 8. Be careful though; the question asks for the length, which is $w + 4 = 12$.

On the SAT, you may see some weird shapes, but don't be intimidated: just break them into familiar shapes!

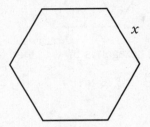

If the area of the regular hexagon above is $54\sqrt{3}$, what is the value of x?

A) 3

B) $2\sqrt{3}$

C) 6

D) 9

A *regular* polygon is one in which all of the side lengths and angles are equal, so every side in this hexagon is equal to x. Also, you know that the length from the vertex to the center is the same for each vertex, and since there are 6 congruent central angles, so each must be 60°. Therefore, you can separate the hexagon into six equilateral triangles as shown on the next page.

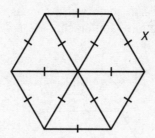

If the area of the whole hexagon is $54\sqrt{3}$, then the area of each equi-

lateral triangle is $\dfrac{54\sqrt{3}}{6} = 9\sqrt{3}$.

Redraw one equilateral triangle and draw the height in. This gives

you two 30-60-90 triangles. Rather than working backwards to solve

for x using the area, you can Plug In the Answers at this point. Start

with (C) instead of (B) because it's an easier number to work with.

The ratio of side lengths in a 30-60-90 triangle are a: $a\sqrt{3}$: $2a$, so if

$x = 6$, then these sides are 3: $3\sqrt{3}$: 6.

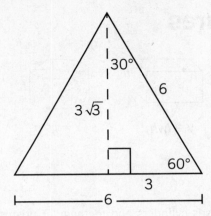

Now, you can solve for the area of this triangle and compare it to the target value of $9\sqrt{3}$.

$A = \dfrac{1}{2}\,bh = \dfrac{1}{2}(6)(3\sqrt{3}) = 9\sqrt{3}$. This matches the target value, so the answer is (C).

3-D Figures

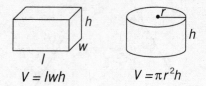

$V = lwh$ $V = \pi r^2 h$

Volume

The SAT often uses cylinders and rectangular prisms to test volume concepts. Take a look at the two questions below:

35

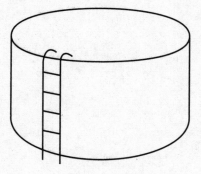

An above-ground pool at a town park is in the shape of a right circular cylinder as shown above. If the pool has a height of 5 feet, and the volume of the pool is 80π cubic feet, what is the diameter of the base of the pool, in feet?

The volume of a right circular cylinder can be found using the formula $V = \pi r^2 h$. Plug in the numbers from the problem and solve for the radius.

$$80\pi = \pi r^2(5)$$
$$16 = r^2$$
$$r = 4$$

Remember that the question asked for the diameter. Since $2r = d$, the diameter is $2 \times 4 = 8$.

33

A certain rectangular prism has a height of z meters, a length that is 2 meters less than its height, and a width that is 3 meters more than its height. If the base of this prism has an area of 36 square meters, what is the volume of the prism, in cubic meters?

Take this one piece at a time:

Height $= z$
Length $= z - 2$
Width $= z + 3$

The base of the prism is a rectangle with a length of $z - 2$ and a width of $z + 3$, so according to the problem, $(z - 2)(z + 3) = 36$. You could solve for the possible values of z algebraically, but it might be easier to test out some possible factors of 36. In this case, you need 2 numbers that multiply out to equal 36, but have a difference of 5. The factors 9 and 4 will work perfectly. If the width $(z + 3) = 9$ and the length $(z - 2) = 4$, then z must equal 6. Plug this back into the dimensions to find the volume of the prism.

Height = 6
Length = 6 − 2 = 4
Width = 6 + 3 = 9
Volume = lwh = (6)(4)(9) = 216.

Surface Area

The surface area of a 3-D figure is the sum of the areas of all of its faces. Consider the rectangular box below.

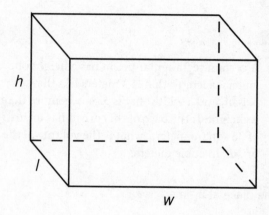

The base and the top of the box are rectangles with an area of lw. The front and the back of the box are rectangles with an area of hw, and the sides facing to the left and the right are rectangles with an area of lh. Therefore, the surface area of a rectangular prism is given by the following formula:

$$SA = 2lw + 2lh + 2hw$$

You can use this same idea to derive a formula for the surface area of a variety of 3-D figures. Determine the area of each face individually, and then find the sum of the areas. For example, the surface area of a cylinder is $SA = 2\pi r^2 + 2\pi rh$ because both the top and bottom of the cylinder are circles with an area of πr^2, and you can think of the surface area of the center of the cylinder as a rectangle with a length equal to the circumference ($2\pi r$) and a height of h. (Think of the cylinder like a can of soup. The label that wraps around the can would have a height of h and a length equal to the circumference of the circle).

Try the following question:

26

The surface area of a cube is $6\left(\dfrac{y}{2}\right)^2$. What is the perimeter of one face of the cube?

A) $\dfrac{y}{2}$

B) y

C) $2y$

D) $4y$

Think about how to find the surface area of a cube. Each side of a cube is a square with an area of s^2, and a cube has 6 sides. This means that $SA = 6s^2 = 6\left(\dfrac{y}{2}\right)^2$. Therefore, the side of each edge of the cube is $\dfrac{y}{2}$. The perimeter of a face is the sum of the 4 edges of that face, so perimeter $= 4\left(\dfrac{y}{2}\right) = 2y$, (C).

Trigonometry

The three basic trigonometry functions are sine, cosine, and tangent. The value of each in a right triangle can be found using the following formulas. An easy way to remember these formulas is with the acronym SOH CAH TOA.

SOH: $\text{Sin} = \dfrac{O}{H}$ $\text{Sine} = \dfrac{opposite}{hypotenuse}$

CAH: $\text{Cos} = \dfrac{A}{H}$ $\text{Cosine} = \dfrac{adjacent}{hypotenuse}$

TOA: $\text{Tan} = \dfrac{O}{A}$ $\text{Tangent} = \dfrac{opposite}{adjacent}$

"Opposite" refers to the side directly across from an angle and "adjacent" refers to the leg next to an angle. The hypotenuse is the longest side and is across from the right angle. The chart below shows the sine, cosine, and tangent, for angles x and y in the triangle below.

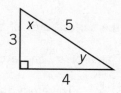

$$\sin(x) = \frac{4}{5} \quad \sin(y) = \frac{3}{5}$$

$$\cos(x) = \frac{3}{5} \quad \cos(y) = \frac{4}{5}$$

$$\tan(x) = \frac{4}{3} \quad \tan(y) = \frac{3}{4}$$

Complementary Angles

Complementary angles are angles that add to 90°. For example, 30° and 60° are complementary angles. Since a triangle has 180°, all right triangles have a 90° angle and a pair of complementary angles. Consider the triangle below. What is the value of sin$A$? What about cos$B$?

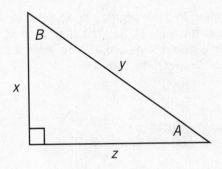

Both of these values are $\dfrac{x}{y}$. In fact, for any complementary angles A and B, sin$A$ = cos$B$. This concept appears frequently on the test. Take a look at the question below:

17

Angle B in right triangle ABC has a measure of $b°$. If the cosine of B is $\dfrac{5}{12}$, what is $\sin(90° - b°)$?

Since complementary angles are two angles that add to 90°, this question is actually asking for the sine of the complementary angle to angle B. Recall that the sine of one angle is equal to the cosine of its complement, so $\sin(90° - b°) = \cos B = \dfrac{5}{12}$.

Converting Radians to Degrees

Angles can be measured in degrees or radians. A full circle has 360° and a radian measure of 2π. You may be asked to convert a radian measure to a degree measure, or vice versa. Use the following formulas to convert between the two:

$$\text{Degrees} = \text{radians} \times \dfrac{180}{\pi}$$

$$\text{Radians} = \text{degrees} \times \dfrac{\pi}{180}$$

For more free content, visit PrincetonReview.com

Your Turn—Exercise 9.1

1. $480° = $ _____ radians

2. $\dfrac{3\pi}{7} = $ _____ degrees

Answers to Exercise 9.1

1. Radians $= 480° \times \dfrac{\pi}{180} = \dfrac{8}{3}\pi$

2. Degrees $= \dfrac{3\pi}{7} \times \dfrac{180}{\pi} = \dfrac{540}{7} \approx 77.1°$

Imaginary Numbers

Consider $\sqrt{-9}$. This doesn't have a real solution because you can't take the square root of a negative number. However, it does have an *imaginary solution*. Imaginary numbers are denoted with an *i*. The main thing you need to keep in mind with imaginary numbers is that $i^2 = -1$. The imaginary solution to $\sqrt{-9}$ is $3i$ because $(3i)^2 = 3^2(i^2) = 9(-1) = -9$.

Take a look at this question:

10

Which of the following complex numbers is equivalent to $\dfrac{6 - 5i}{2 - 4i}$?

A) $\dfrac{8}{5} - \dfrac{7i}{10}$

B) $\dfrac{8}{5} + \dfrac{7i}{10}$

C) $\dfrac{2}{5} + \dfrac{7i}{10}$

D) $\dfrac{2}{5} - \dfrac{7i}{10}$

This expression has a complex number in both the numerator and denominator. A complex number is a number that has both a real component and an imaginary component. It is written in the form $a + bi$, in which the a is the real part of the number and the bi is the imaginary component. To simplify this you need to get rid of the imaginary number in the denominator by multiplying by the *conjugate*. A *conjugate* of a binomial flips the sign of the second term. The conjugate of $2 - 4i$ is $2 + 4i$. You also need to multiply the numerator by the same thing to avoid changing the value of the expression.

$$\frac{6 - 5i}{2 - 4i} \times \frac{2 + 4i}{2 + 4i} = \frac{(6 - 5i)(2 + 4i)}{4 - 16i^2} = \frac{12 + 24i - 10i - 20i^2}{4 - 16i^2}$$

Now you can replace the i^2 terms with (-1):

$$\frac{12 + 14i - 20(-1)}{4 - (-16)} = \frac{32 + 14i}{20}$$

You can then split this fraction into two to match the format of the answer choices:

$$\frac{32}{20} + \frac{14i}{20} = \frac{8}{5} + \frac{7i}{10}$$

The answer is (B).

Your Turn—Exercise 9.2

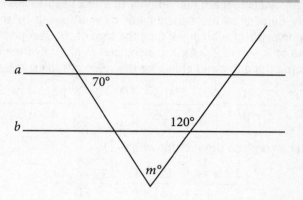

In the figure above, lines *a* and *b* are parallel. What is the value of *m* ?

A) 35

B) 50

C) 60

D) 90

5

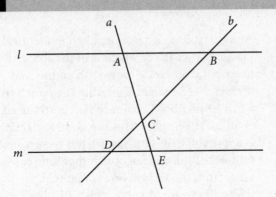

Lines *l* and *m*, shown above, are parallel. Lines *a* and *b* intersect as shown. If segment *DE* is 12, *CE* is 6, and *AC* is 18, what is the length of *AB*?

A)   9

B)   18

C)   24

D)   36

6

What is the value of $(3 + 4i)(3 - 4i)$?

A)   1

B)   5

C)   9

D)   25

18

At a party, Kate is serving punch in identical plastic cups, each of which is in the shape of a right circular cylinder with an internal diameter of 3 inches. She ladles the punch from a full 10-liter bowl into each cup until the cup is full. If the height of the punch in each cup is approximately 4 inches, what is the greatest number of full cups of punch that Kate can serve from the 10-liter bowl of punch?
(Note: There are 61 cubic inches in 1 liter).

A)   5

B)   16

C)   21

D)   22

19

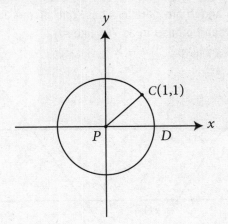

In the xy-plane above, P is the center of the circle and the measure of $\angle CPD$ is $\dfrac{\pi}{c}$ radians. What is the value of c ?

Answers and Explanations to Exercise 9.2

2. **B** Since *a* and *b* are parallel lines, one of the angles in the triangle can be filled in as 70° like so:

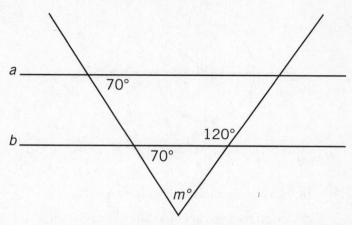

The other angle in the triangle is 60° since it is supplementary to the 120° angle:

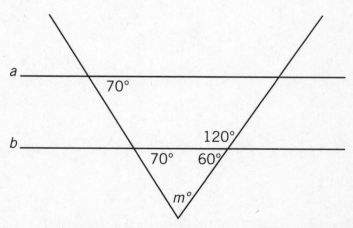

There are 180° in a triangle, so 180° − 70° − 60° = 50° = *m*.

For more free content, visit PrincetonReview.com

5. **D** $\angle ABC$ is equal to $\angle CDE$ because they are formed by line b intersecting two parallel lines. Angles BAC and CED are equal for the same reason. The two opposite angles at point C are equal, so triangles CDE and ABC are similar. Set up a proportion: $\frac{12}{6} = \frac{x}{18}$. When you solve for x, you find that AB is 36.

6. **D** Use FOIL to multiply the expression to get $9 - 12i + 12i - 16i^2$. Since $i^2 = -1$, and the two $12i$'s cancel out, you are left with $9 + 16$, which is 25.

18. **B** Start off by finding the volume of each full cup using the formula $V = \pi r^2 h$. Remember that 3 inches is the diameter, so 1.5 inches is the radius.

    $V = \pi(1.5)^2(4) = 28.27$ cubic inches

    Now find the total volume of the punch bowl. Since the bowl is 10 liters, the total volume is $61 \times 10 = 610$ cubic inches. This needs to be divided by the volume of each cup:

    $\frac{610}{28.27} = 21.58$ cups

    Since the question specifically asks how many FULL cups of punch Kate will be able to serve, the answer is (C), 21. There is not enough punch to fill up a 22nd cup.

19. **4** The best way to solve this is to use the coordinates of point C to draw a triangle like so:

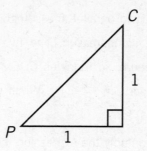

You should recognize that this is an isosceles right triangle with angle measurements of 45°-45°-90°. Therefore, angle *P* is 45°. This needs to be converted to radians. Remember that radians = degrees × $\frac{\pi}{180°}$:

$$45° \times \frac{\pi}{180°} = \frac{\pi}{4} \qquad c = 4$$

Key Terms

This Key Terms section is a list of some of the challenging words you might see in Reading passages.

Some people like using flash cards to learn vocabulary. If this works for you, do so. Another great way to learn words is to take a few words every day and use them at every opportunity. You will probably annoy your friends, but you will certainly learn these words.

In addition to learning these words, try to read as much as you can. While you're reading, note the words you don't know and look them up in a dictionary.

Acute   sensitive; sharp; discerning
His hearing was unusually acute.

Adept   very skilled
Eloise became adept at drawing a straight line without the use of the ruler.

Ambivalent   simultaneously feeling opposing feelings; uncertain
Amy felt ambivalent about her dance class: on one hand, she enjoyed the exercise; but on the other, the choice of dances bored her.

Analogy   a comparison
Early internet developers created an analogy between viral infections and the popularity of video clips.

Anecdote   a short account of an interesting incident
My uncle Richard is known for his many stories and childhood anecdotes.

Anomaly   something that is abnormal or irregular
James is an anomaly; he is equally skilled in both art and science.

Apprehensive   fearful about the future
My grandmother was very apprehensive before her hernia surgery.

Brevity the quality or state of being brief in duration
Brevity = briefness. (You can't get any shorter than that!)

Candor completely honest, straightforward
Candace's candidness overwhelmed her business colleagues, who were not used to such honesty.

Complacent satisfied with the current situation and unconcerned with changing it
Voter turnout is chronically low in this city; many residents are complacent about the current state of politics.

Conspicuous easy to notice; obvious (antonym: inconspicuous)
The red tuxedo was conspicuous among all the classic black ones. What was he thinking?

Deference submission or courteous respect
The children were taught to show deference to their parents.

Denounce to condemn openly
In many powerful speeches throughout his lifetime, Martin Luther King, Jr. denounced racism as immoral.

Despondent depressed
The despondent supporters of the defeated candidate gasped when he announced that he would suspend his campaign indefinitely.

Disdain to regard with contempt
The critics disdained the new author for his lack of skill.

Disparage to speak of negatively; to belittle
Wanda disparaged Glen by calling him a cheat and a liar.

Diversion something that distracts the mind or entertains
For many bored teenagers, Instagram is a worthwhile diversion.

Dubious   doubtful; of unlikely authenticity
Jerry's dubious claim that he could fly like Superman didn't win him any summer job offers.

Earnest   expressing sincerity
Jack's offer to help Diane was an earnest gesture of goodwill.

Empirical   derived from observation or experiment
The young medical researcher was sincerely hoping for empirical results that would support his hypothesis.

Erratic   markedly inconsistent
Erroll's erratic behavior made it difficult for his friends to predict what he would do in a given moment.

Evoke   to summon or draw forth
His suspicious behavior at the airport evoked mistrust in the security guards.

Explicit   fully and clearly expressed
You do not have permission to stay at your friend's house without your mother's explicit approval.

Frank   open and sincere
Maureen's teacher made several frank remarks about the quality of her work.

Hypothesis   a possible but unproven explanation
Dr. Warren's hypothesis regarding the existence of alien life forms has yet to be proven.

Implicit   implied
Mark and his mother had an implicit agreement not to discuss his failures at work.

Indifferent   having no interest or concern
We should never be indifferent to the suffering of others.

Indignation   anger aroused by something perceived as unjust
The presidential candidate won by expressing indignation about the failing economy.

Innovation   the act of introducing something new; a new idea, device, or method
The computer industry has succeeded by implementing a series of successful innovations.

Lament   to mourn
Jessica lamented the death of her grandfather.

Malicious   deliberately harmful
We tried not to listen to the malicious gossip being spread about the new science teacher.

Malleable   capable of being shaped
Aluminum is a malleable metal appropriate for many industrial uses.

Mediation   a settlement between conflicting parties
John's father is a lawyer who specializes in the mediation of labor-management disputes.

Nostalgia   a bittersweet longing for things of the past
Katrina was often nostalgic for her hometown in rural Kansas.

Novel (adj)   fresh; original; new
It was a novel idea, the sort of thing no one had tried before.

Obscure (adj.)   not readily noticed; vague
Some say that James Joyce's writing style is obscure and complex.

Objective (adj.)   uninfluenced by emotions
Judges are expected to make objective decisions unaffected by their personal biases.

Ominous   menacing; threatening
The tornado was preceded by ominous black clouds for as far as the eye could see.

Pervade   to be present throughout
The sweet scent of lilacs pervaded the garden.

Provocative   giving rise to action or feeling
The senator's provocative comments sparked an uproar among even his staunchest supporters.

Prudent   careful; wise
Dan became a millionaire after a lifetime of prudent investments.

Reciprocate   to mutually take or give; to respond in kind
The chef reciprocated his rival's respect; they admired each other so much that they even traded recipes.

Recount   to describe
The historian's book skillfully recounts the Battle of Normandy.

Resignation   unresisting acceptance; submission
Tim shrugged with resignation after losing his third tennis match in one week.

Substantiate   to support with proof or evidence; verify
The argument was substantiated by clear facts and hard evidence.

Superficial   near the surface; shallow; unimportant
Despite the hype surrounding the second edition of the book, it contained only superficial changes.

Tactful   considerate and discreet
A tactful remark can diffuse even the most tense of disagreements.

Undermine   to weaken

A lack of sleep can undermine one's health and happiness.

Underscore   to put emphasis on

The rising price of fuel underscored the need for greater efficiencies.

NOTES

NOTES

NOTES

NOTES

NOTES

NOTES

NOTES

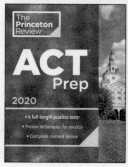